TIME
ANNUAL
2011

Why me? *This Gulf Coast native, its feathers fouled by oil leaking from the Deepwater Horizon well, was taken from Louisiana's Barataria Bay to be cleaned up. The well leaked for 86 days*

TIME

MANAGING EDITOR Richard Stengel
ART DIRECTOR D.W. Pine

TIME ANNUAL 2011

EDITOR Kelly Knauer
DESIGNER Ellen Fanning
PICTURE EDITOR Patricia Cadley
RESEARCH Tresa McBee
COPY EDITOR Bruce Christopher Carr

TIME HOME ENTERTAINMENT
PUBLISHER Richard Fraiman
GENERAL MANAGER Steven Sandonato
EXECUTIVE DIRECTOR, MARKETING SERVICES Carol Pittard
DIRECTOR, RETAIL AND SPECIAL SALES Tom Mifsud
DIRECTOR, NEW PRODUCT DEVELOPMENT Peter Harper
DIRECTOR, BOOKAZINE DEVELOPMENT AND MARKETING Laura Adam
PUBLISHING DIRECTOR, BRAND MARKETING Joy Butts
ASSOCIATE GENERAL COUNSEL Helen Wan
BOOK PRODUCTION MANAGER Suzanne Janso
DESIGN AND PREPRESS MANAGER Anne-Michelle Gallero
BRAND MANAGER Michela Wilde
ASSOCIATE PREPRESS MANAGER Alex Voznesenskiy

SPECIAL THANKS TO:
Christine Austin, Jeremy Biloon, Glenn Buonocore, Jim Childs, Susan Chodakiewicz, Rose Cirrincione, Brian Fellows, Jacqueline Fitzgerald, Carrie Frazier, Lauren Hall, Brynn Joyce, Mona Li, Robert Marasco, Kimberly Marshall, Amy Migliaccio, Brooke Reger, Dave Rozzelle, Ilene Schreider, Adriana Tierno, TIME Imaging, Sydney Webber

ISBN 10: 1-60320-869-0
ISBN 13: 978-1-60320-869-7
ISSN: 1097-5721

Published by TIME Books, an imprint of Time Home Entertainment, Inc.
135 W. 50th Street, New York, NY 10020

We welcome your comments and suggestions about TIME Books. Please write to us at:
TIME Books, Attention: Book Editors, P.O. Box 11016, Des Moines, IA 50336-1016

To order any of our hardcover Collector's Edition books, please call us at 1-800-327-6388.
Hours: Monday through Friday, 7 a.m.–8 p.m., or Saturday, 7 a.m.– 6 p.m., Central Time.

To enjoy TIME's real-time coverage of the news, visit: **time.com**

Sign language *Sergeant Kevin Garcia of Colorado Springs, Colo., has a message for locals while on patrol with the 4th Brigade Special Troops Battalion in Afghanistan's Nangarhar province on March 11*

JULIE JACOBSON—AP IMAGES

Contents

Looking up *Switzerland's Simon Ammann takes a gold medal in ski jumping at the Winter Olympic Games in Canada*

Images

All Fouled Up

Only five years after Hurricane Katrina slammed into the U.S. Gulf Coast, another catastrophe struck the region. This time around, the tragedy was man-made rather than natural: when an oil rig exploded and a deep undersea well began gushing petroleum into the Gulf, the well's owner, British Petroleum, took three months to contain the spill, and an estimated 5 million barrels of oil leaked into the Gulf. At left, the plumage of a brown pelican, Louisiana's state bird, is coated with crude oil.

Mood indigo *A ship traversing the Gulf of Mexico finds its crystal-blue waters are bisected by dark plumes of oil leaking from the wellhead beneath*

the Deepwater Horizon oil rig, which exploded on April 20, then burned and sank. The leaking well was not capped until July 15

Free at last *Florencio Avalos, left, shares a hug with Chile's President, Sebastián Piñera, after being rescued from the San José mine on Oct. 13. Av*

s the first of 33 miners trapped deep underground for 69 days to be rescued, brought to the surface in the escape capsule at left

Deus ex machina *Pakistanis seeking food and fresh water stretch to reach aid supplies delived by a hovering helicopter in the wake of the massive flo*

struck the nation in July and August, after heavy monsoon rains. An estimated 18 to 20 million people were left dead, injured or homeless

Aftermath *Mac Fanieh of Port-au-Prince struggles to extricate himself from the rubble left by a major earthquake that struck Haiti on Jan. 12, leavin*

250,000 dead. Fanieh had dug into a collapsed school, passing the deceased student at right, in hopes of rescuing a teacher trapped alive

Elevation *In the final match of soccer's 2010 World Cup, goaltender Iker Casillas of Spain goes airborne—and then some—to take the ball out of p*

Robin van Persie of the Netherlands, in orange, looks on, and Carles Puyol of Spain slides beneath him. Spain won the game, 1-0

Primal forces *Lightning cracks above the Eyjafjallajokull volcano in Iceland, where small-scale activity that began in 2009 gave way to large*

eruptions in April, sending giant clouds of ash across European skies. Electrical discharges within the ash column spark the lightning

Verbatim 2010

'Your face tells a story—and it shouldn't be a story about your drive to the doctor's office.'

JULIA ROBERTS, on saying no to Botox

'Rich people spend a lot more money on their own problems, like baldness, than they do to fight malaria.'

BILL GATES, criticizing Italy's low levels of foreign aid in 2009—which had fallen by half from the year before—and blaming Prime Minister Silvio Berlusconi, who is rumored to have undergone hair transplants

'I think, the Vatican—they've got more to talk about than the Beatles.'

RINGO STARR, responding to a Vatican newspaper editorial that praised the band on the 40th anniversary of its breakup

'I never considered myself a maverick.'

JOHN MCCAIN, rejecting a label on which he campaigned for the presidency in 2008

'I was also going to give a graduation speech in Arizona this weekend, but with my accent, I was afraid they would try to deport me.'

ARNOLD SCHWARZENEGGER, governor of California, ribbing Arizona's new immigration law during his commencement speech at Emory University in Atlanta

'I'm living proof that you can survive without sex for that long.'

JIM GIBBONS, Nevada governor, saying he has not been intimate with any woman, including his wife, since 1995, in his deposition in a civil suit filed by a woman who charged him with battery, false imprisonment and other alleged misdeeds

'A ban on eating them would show China has reached a new level of civilization.'

CHANG JIWEN, a professor at the Chinese Academy of the Social Sciences, on the Chinese government's consideration of legislation that would make eating cats and dogs illegal

'Many women who do not dress modestly lead young men astray, corrupt their chastity and spread adultery in society, which increases earthquakes.'

HOJATOLESLAM KAZEM SEDIGHI, an Iranian Muslim cleric, blaming women for a spate of temblors around the globe early in 2010

'This microbe is really a very hard worker.'

GARY HEBL, a Wisconsin state representative who submitted a bill to name *Lactococcus lactis*, the bacterium used to make a number of cheeses, the official state microbe

'Dude, you have no Koran!'

JACOB ISOM, a resident of Amarillo, Texas, on what he said after snatching Islam's holy book from the leader of a local Christian group intent on burning it in protest

'This is a big f__ing deal.'

VICE PRESIDENT JOE BIDEN, sotto voce, to Barack Obama at the signing into law of the Administration's historic health-care reform bill

'We don't trample the livelihood of those we're trying to win over.'

COMMANDER JEFFREY EGGERS, a top adviser to General Stanley McChrystal, on the reluctance of U.S. and NATO commanders to eradicate opium crops in Marjah; the stance is part of an effort to win over Afghans residing in former Taliban territory

'They're better on his desk than on my chest.'

SHARON OSBOURNE, reality-television veteran, on her plan to remove her breast implants and give them to her husband Ozzy Osbourne to use as paperweights

'We used to hustle on over the border for health care … And I think, Isn't that kind of ironic now?'

SARAH PALIN, former governor of Alaska, admitting that her family used to go to Canada for medical treatment when she was a child; Canada has a single-payer system, which Palin opposes

'Did you plug the hole yet, Daddy?'

MALIA OBAMA, per the President, who said his daughter interrupted him while he was shaving to inquire about the status of the Gulf oil spill

'Presidents get swollen heads.'

SAYED HABIB SADAT, Afghan hatmaker, on President Hamid Karzai's signature karakul hat, whose measurements have increased an inch since Karzai took office

Sandip Roy

Describing the new colonialism that underlies Eat, Pray, Love *on* **Salon.com:**

"I couldn't help wondering, where do these people in Indonesia and India go away to when they lose their passion, spark and faith? I don't think they come to Manhattan. I wonder if there could be an exchange program for the passion-deprived, a sort of global spark-swap." —8/13/10

Con Coughlin

Writing in the **Telegraph** *about the precarious situation in Pakistan:*

"If ever a country were ripe for a coup, it is Pakistan. The besieged government of President Asif Ali Zardari is assailed on all fronts by man-made conflict and natural disaster, and there is a palpable sense in Islamabad that the return of the generals to the presidential palace would come as something of a relief."
—8/25/10

Scott Mendelson

Reflecting on Kathryn Bigelow's historic win of the Oscar for Best Director for her film The Hurt Locker, *on the* **Huffington Post:**

"She was absolutely deserving … Not because she's a woman and not because she's a woman who makes stereotypically 'guy' movies, but because *The Hurt Locker* was a damn good movie and she was the primary reason it worked … The fact that it took 82 years for the Academy to give the Best Director award to a female filmmaker should be a cause for shame and embarrassment rather than self-lionizing accolades." —3/8/10

In the Limelight. A hunky huckster, a talkative general and a snarky flight attendant kept us buzzing

Bride of the Year

One clue this wasn't any old wedding: the FAA deemed the airspace over Rhinebeck, N.Y., a no-fly zone on July 31, the day when former First Daughter Chelsea Clinton, 30, wed New York City investment banker Marc Mezvinsky, 32. The interfaith service was held at Astor Courts, a 50-acre 1902 Beaux Arts estate on a bluff overlooking the Hudson River, owned by a friend of the bride's mother, Secretary of State Hillary Clinton. Although some 400 people attended, the event had a family feeling, many guests reported. The bride wore Vera Wang; she and father Bill Clinton shared a dance to *The Way You Look Tonight*.

Best-Smelling Man of the Year

In America's ad-saturated society, it takes a heck of a commercial to stand out. But the folks at Old Spice and their ad agency, Wieden+Kennedy, broke away from the pack with their nifty videos, filmed in single, hard-to-believe takes, which quickly achieved marketing Nirvana, 2010-style: they went viral on the Internet and were viewed, parodied and envied millions of times. The breakout star of the commercials was former pro footballer Isaiah Mustafa—and yes, ladies, he definitely looks better than your man.

SMELL LIKE A MAN, MAN.
Old Spice

Offspring of The Year

Bristol Palin, daughter of former Alaska Governor Sarah Palin, kept herself in the headlines, most prominently as a contestant on ABC's *Dancing with the Stars*, right. She also declared she would marry Levi Johnston, the father of her child, but called it off after a few days, saying, "He's just obsessed with the limelight, and I got played."

Retirees of the Year

No, "longtime" isn't their first name, but we can be forgiven for thinking so. For a longtime radio host, a longtime Supreme Court justice and a longtime White House correspondent, 2010 was the year when they finally hung it up.

LARRY KING

Age: 76

Job: Host, CNN's prime-time talk show *Larry King Live*

Years of service: 25

Reason: "… more time for my [seventh] wife and to get to the kids' Little League baseball games."

JUSTICE J.P. STEVENS

Age: 90

Job: Justice, Supreme Court

Years of service: 34

Reason: It was time. "If I have overstayed my welcome, it is because this is such a unique and wonderful job."

HELEN THOMAS

Age: 89

Job: White House correspondent

Years of service: 57

Reason: The Lebanese American stepped down after stating that Israeli Jews should "get the hell out of Palestine."

Wonder Woman of the Year

Giving Lady Gaga a run for her money was outré pop star Katy Perry, née Katy Hudson, a onetime gospel singer whose good cheer, wacky costumes and carefully calibrated songs, like the 2010 hit *California Gurls,* recorded with Snoop Dogg, won her a No. 1 album—and the heart of another ace at playing the media, British actor Russell Brand.

Hissy Fit of The Year

JetBlue flight attendant Steven Slater achieved folk-hero status when, after an altercation with a passenger, he cursed her out over the PA, then deplaned to the tarmac, with a beer in hand, via the emergency slide.

Teen Idol of the Year

Fresh-faced Canadian songbird Justin Bieber, who turned 16 in 2010, rose to fame by imitating soulful singers on YouTube. In 2010 he was named Best New Artist on the MTV Music Video Awards, where he performed his chart-topping (and somewhat self-descriptive) hit *Baby*. Asked his Valentine plans, he hit just the right note: "I have one person that I'll be sending flowers to, and that's my mom."

Loose Lips of the Year

You'd expect that the Pentagon's top man in Afghanistan would have learned discretion during his stellar 34-year career. But you'd be wrong in the case of General Stanley McChrystal, who was quoted saying disparaging things about members of the Obama Administration in a *Rolling Stone* magazine interview and was quickly canned by the President. Next step: a teaching gig at Yale University.

17

Nation

Election 2010

They were mad as hell—and the Tea Party activists who converged on Washington on April 15 wanted everyone to know it. Their vehement denunciations of both Republicans and Democrats echoed the mood of a disgruntled nation, as TIME political analyst Joe Klein reported after traveling 6,782 miles on a coast-to-coast road trip that brought him in close contact with everyday Americans.

Voters, Klein found, "tended to be more anxious than angry ... [they were] extremely frustrated with the national conversation as presented by the news media. There was a unanimous sense that Washington was broken beyond repair."

On Nov. 2, U.S. voters put Republicans in charge of the House of Representatives but not the Senate, and the scene was set for a period of divided government. And now the nation faced a new question: Could an emboldened GOP work with a Democratic President to bring about the change Americans so earnestly desired?

Changing Course

Frustrated Americans send a firm message—and a flock of new Republicans—to Washington

VOTERS HIT THE RESET BUTTON ON AMERICAN politics on Tuesday, Nov. 2. When the dust settled, there would be no more Speaker of the House Nancy Pelosi, no more one-party control of the Federal Government, no more Obama landslide map. The next day the country was still facing all the same problems—but the menu of solutions was up for grabs. "Yes, we can" had collided with "Oh, no you don't." And the starter's gun had fired on the future—including the 2012 presidential election.

The swing voters who flocked to Barack Obama in 2008 turned against his agenda, electing a tidal wave of new Republican members of Congress, and shaving the Democratic advantage in the Senate to a hair's breadth. Perhaps the night's biggest winner was House minority leader John Boehner of the GOP, now in line to become the next Speaker. "The American people have sent an unmistakable message to [the President] tonight," Boehner declared at a victory party, "and that message is, 'Change course.'"

As the number of House seats captured by the GOP reached 60, Democrats pondered a loss of historic scope, well exceeding the 52 seats captured by the GOP in the 1994 Gingrich revolution. Exit polls suggested that widespread anger over the government's handling of the poor economy was the fuel that fed the firestorm—it was a wave of discontent, a resounding vote of no confidence in all branches of power.

One observer who agreed with that analysis was the President. In a White House press conference on the afternoon of Nov. 3, a chastened Obama said, "There is no doubt that people's No.1 concern is the economy." Admitting that "some election nights are more fun than others," he acknowledged that the Democrats had taken a beating and promised he would work harder to build consensus, calling repeatedly for the two parties to work together for the good of the nation.

As Democrats climb from the rubble of their defeat, they will notice that the results could have been even worse. The key building blocks of liberal election strategy—New York and California—resisted the GOP tide. And they will notice, no doubt, that the seeds of future squabbles were sown inside the enemy camps.

Tea Party insurgents forced the nomination of weak, extreme candidates in several key races. The price of those primary victories proved very high in the general election. Right-wing purists squandered Republican chances to control the Senate, to defeat Senate majority leader Harry Reid of Nevada and to elect a governor in the swing state of Colorado.

The White House had plenty of opportunity to brace

We, the people *From Alaska to New York, Americans went to the polls on Nov. 2 in a heated—and historic—midterm election*

for the loss of the House. Indeed, many Democratic strategists were saying bravely as the blowout approached that Obama would be better off without Pelosi as Speaker, free to operate with only his own interests and agenda to consider. Having the Republicans in charge of at least one chamber of Congress, the thinking went, could give the President fresh room to maneuver.

But that was happy talk compared with the changes the results will force in Obama's re-election plans. If you take the President's 2008 victory map and subtract the states

where his fellow Democrats were obliterated in major races in 2010—Virginia, Indiana, Ohio, Pennsylvania, Michigan, Wisconsin, Florida—you discover that Obama's 2008 landslide evaporates into a dead heat.

Not only did the Republican Party take power in the House—it also moved to the right within its own ranks, pushed by antitax, antigovernment, anticompromise members of the Tea Party movement. A leader of the movement and winner of the Kentucky Senate campaign, Rand Paul delivered that call to action in his acceptance speech.

New balance *Boehner enjoyed his victory on election night, while Obama called for cooperation in a Nov. 3 press conference*

"I have a message ... that is loud and clear, that does not mince words: We've come to take our government back," Paul told his supporters. "The American people are unhappy with what's going on in Washington." Paul promised them "fiscal sanity," limited constitutional government and balanced budgets.

It was a night on which even the GOP losers felt like bragging. "The Delaware political system will never be the same," crowed Christine O'Donnell, fresh from a 16-point shellacking at the hands of Democratic nominee for U.S. Senate Chris Coons.

In the wake of the election, many political insiders took a hard look at the O'Donnell blowout and wondered why such a weak candidate had the robust backing of the Tea Party insurgents. Did Sarah Palin and South Carolina Senator Jim DeMint, darlings of the Tea Party conservatives, cost the party a shot at control of the Senate when they endorsed a lightweight rather than popular Delaware Congressman Mike Castle?

But the potential bloodletting inside the resurgent GOP is nothing compared with the blame game facing the Democrats. Some will say the President and Congress tried to do too much—bailing out banks, spending some $800 billion on stimulus and pet liberal projects, reorga-

nizing the health-care and auto industries. Some will say they did too little, leaving nearly 10% of the workforce unemployed.

What's clear is that the Obama Administration has lost—at least for now—swing districts and moderate voters. Formerly robust, long-serving conservative Democrats were ousted in the voting: House Armed Services Committee chairman Ike Skelton of Missouri, House Budget chairman John Spratt of South Carolina, House Energy Subcommittee chairman Rick Boucher of Virginia, and others—wiped out.

True, the results were somewhat less dire for the Democrats than the apocalyptic projections widely heard in the final days of the campaign. But with GOP victories seeping down into governors' mansions and state legislatures—and those officials controlling the every-10-years process of drawing new election boundaries—the painful reality could not be avoided. Democrats held some important seats, but they sure didn't gain many. Mostly, they lost ground. Lots of ground.

Just how much ground can be measured by the key Senate election of 2010: the fight to take the late Senator Robert Byrd's West Virginia Senate seat. Governor Joe Manchin III saved the Senate for the Democrats by winning this race—but he managed to win the race only by strongly distancing himself from Obama. He promised to repeal parts of the health-care reform—"overreaching," he said of the bill. And he literally put a bullet in climate-change legislation, airing an ad that showed him chambering a cartridge, shouldering his rifle and blasting a bullet right through the controversial cap-and-trade bill.

Florida, America's New Bellwether State

If any state illustrates the screeching U-turn that American politics has taken in two short years, it's Florida. In the 2008 presidential election, Sunshine State voters made Barack Obama the first Northern Democrat to win the peninsula since Franklin Roosevelt did it in 1944—and a big reason was their desire for the more pragmatic, less partisan leadership they prized in their Governor, moderate Republican Charlie Crist. But on Nov. 2, Floridians like Carlo Sanchez made it clear why they'd just dumped Crist for the more conservative Marco Rubio in the marquee race for the state's open U.S. Senate seat.

"Crist likes to drive all over the political landscape, wherever he thinks he can gain a political advantage," said Sanchez, 67, a retired Miami customs broker sporting a classic Ernest Hemingway beard and a blue guayabera shirt as he waited for Rubio, Florida's former house speaker, to arrive at the ornate Biltmore Hotel to give his victory speech. "Marco on the other hand has always driven straight. He's a real righteous guy, a real conservative. That's what people want right now."

In Florida, America's new bellwether state, that wasn't just the direction voters picked in the Senate race—where Republican Rubio, the 39-year-old son of Cuban exiles, routed Crist, who last spring bolted the GOP to run as an independent, 49% to 30%—but in just about every important congressional contest. Those included the one in the 22nd District, won by Allen West, who will be the state's first African-American Republican to go to Congress since Reconstruction. In the gubernatorial election, controversial Republican Rick Scott won with a razor-slim edge, 49% to 48%, over Democrat Alex Sink. As former Florida Governor and alpha Republican Jeb Bush said, the state's voters were looking for "principle-centered" conservatives who won't "rely on this oppressive [Federal] Government to solve our problems for us."

No Florida victor exemplified that anti-Obama turn to the right more than Jeb's protégé, Rubio, already touted by supporters as a presidential candidate for 2016. Rubio's improbable primary election challenge against Crist, who infuriated the right in 2009 by embracing Obama's $787 billion economic stimulus program (and by hugging Obama himself at a stimulus rally) was the first real cause célèbre for the conservative, anti-Big Government Tea Party movement, which so dramatically and so angrily influenced these midterm elections. Rubio fended off Crist's independent candidacy by smartly avoiding the Tea Party radicalism that catapulted him to the nomination but ultimately tripped up other Tea Party candidates like Sharron Angle in Nevada.

In the end, Rubio even outpolled Crist among Florida's large cache of independent voters, who make up a fifth of the electorate, 48% to 37%. And in an economically battered state that this year registered its worst unemploy-

Rubio's big win *Florida's new Senator may help the GOP reach out to Hispanic voters, badly needed by the party*

Senate
47-53

Republicans picked up six seats but did not take control of the Senate, and the stage seemed set for a period of gridlock in the chamber.

House
240-190 (5)

Republicans won 61 new seats to take firm control of the House, where 218 seats constitutes a majority. Five races were undecided as of Nov. 23.

Governors
29-19-1 (1)

Republicans picked up 7 new governorships to dominate the nation's statehouses. Minnesota's race was undecided as of Nov. 23.

ment rate ever, topping 12%, he even picked up Democrats like Marcia Friedman, a Miami business consultant who showed up at the Biltmore. "I just felt like Rubio heard the pain, realized the trouble the country's in," she said. "His values had a stronger voice for voters like me this time."

Still, even though Rubio is the Republican golden boy this time, he made it clear, as so many other Tea Party-fueled politicians around the country have, that his own party's establishment has been wayward. "This election is not about an embrace of the Republican Party," Rubio told the Biltmore crowd. "It's a second chance for Republicans to be what they said they were going to be not so long ago." That is, the party of smaller solutions and lower spending. He added: "Our nation is headed in the wrong direction and both parties are to blame."

Will Obama Move to the Center?

What comes next is anyone's guess. Can we take heart from the fact that Florida's mouthiest Congressman, freshman Alan Grayson, was trounced after calling his opponent "Taliban Dan" in an egregious television ad? Can we find hope in the fact that a surging politician—the early Tea Party adopter Rubio—can still get away, in this climate, with calling his campaign-trail foes "gracious … worthy opponents"?

Probably not. The election of 2010, momentous as it was, marks the beginning of a bigger battle—not the end. It also presents President Obama with a fresh opportunity. The Republican Party won the midterms by moving to the right. That leaves the rest of the spectrum wide open. If Obama can settle his differences with moderate voters, and seize ownership of the middle ground, he will find a lot of the electorate waiting patiently for him.

In the long run, the story of huge midterms losses is shelved in the library of political campaigns right next to the tale of presidential comebacks: just consult the history books on the rebuffs dealt to Ronald Reagan in 1982 and Bill Clinton in 1994. Barack Obama lived through the first edition, and now he must try to create the sequel. ∎

> **"Some elections are more fun than others. Some are exhilarating. Some are humbling … There is no doubt that people's No. 1 concern is the economy."**
>
> —BARACK OBAMA

Election 2010

Republicans Take Control of the House.
But the red tide did not extend to the Senate

THE MIDTERM ELECTIONS WERE a bracing victory for the GOP, as Republicans took a firm majority in the House. But Democrats held on to a majority in the Senate, aided by the losses of two Tea Party candidates who ousted more mainstream Republicans in Delaware and Nevada in the primaries. In the nation's statehouses, troubled by fiscal woes, the GOP also outpaced the Democrats.

Nevada SENATE

SHARRON ANGLE
Republican
45%

✓**HARRY REID**
Democrat
50%

Delaware SENATE

CHRISTINE O'DONNELL
Republican
40%

✓**CHRIS COONS**
Democrat
57%

California SENATE

CARLY FIORINA
Republican
42%

✓**BARBARA BOXER**
Democrat
52%

Arkansas SENATE

✓**JOHN BOOZMAN**
Republican
58%

BLANCHE LINCOLN
Democrat
37%

Missouri SENATE

✓**ROY BLUNT**
Republican
54%

ROBIN CARNAHAN
Democrat
41%

Wisconsin SENATE

✓**RON JOHNSON**
Republican
52%

RUSS FEINGOLD
Democrat
47%

New York GOVERNOR

CARL PALADINO
Republican
34%

✓**ANDREW CUOMO**
Democrat
62%

California GOVERNOR

MEG WHITMAN
Republican
41%

✓**JERRY BROWN**
Democrat
54%

When Hope Met Reality

Barack Obama was sworn into the presidency amid a tide of hope for the future. Where did all that adoration go?

THERE'S GOT TO BE A MORNING AFTER. AND ON Nov. 3, President Barack Obama faced his: the day after the 2010 midterm elections, in a White House press conference, Obama admitted that his party had taken a "shellacking," and he took the blame upon himself. The President conceded that his relationship with the American people "has gotten rockier and tougher" over the last two years, as America's recession dragged on.

What happened to Obama's promise of change? Nine weeks before the midterm elections, TIME's Michael Scherer visited Indiana and filed a story that captured the mood of the nation as the elections approached. A dozen miles west of Elkhart, Scherer watched as hundreds gathered in a school gym for a job fair. With the local unemployment rate above 12% and rising again in the summer, about a third of the employer display tables stood empty. Julie Griffin, who voted for Obama in 2008, sat down at the room's edge, well dressed and discouraged. After 23 years as a payroll administrator at a local RV plant, she was laid off 18 months before. "Really, what has he been doing?" she said when Scherer asked about Obama's efforts to help people like her. "I guess I don't know what he is doing."

Across the gym floor, Joe Donnelly, Elkhart's pro-life, pro-gun Democratic Congressman, worked the crowd. He was part of the moderate wave that won Congress for Nancy Pelosi in 2006, and he was re-elected with 67% of the vote while campaigning for Obama in 2008. The President had since returned to the region three times, but

Donnelly was nonetheless fighting for his political life. In a recent television ad, an unflattering photo of Obama and Pelosi flashes while Donnelly condemns "the Washington crowd." This became a Democratic campaign slogan: Don't blame me for Obama and Pelosi. "I'm not one of them," Donnelly told Scherer. "I'm one of us." (Apparently so: he was re-elected in November.)

This shift in perception—from Obama as political savior to Obama as creature of Washington—could be seen elsewhere. When Obama arrived in office in January 2009, his Gallup approval rating stood at 68%, a high for a newly elected leader not seen since John Kennedy in 1961. In September 2010, Obama's job approval was hovering in the mid-40s, which meant that at least 1 in 4 Americans had changed his or her mind. The plunge had been particularly dramatic among independents, whites and those under age 30. Instead of the generational transformation some Democrats predicted after 2008, the President's party was clearly teetering on the brink of the broad setback it would suffer in November.

White House aides explained this change as a largely inevitable reflection of the cycles of history. Midterms almost always go badly for first-term Presidents, and worse in hard times. "The public is rightly frustrated and angry with the economy," said Dan Pfeiffer, Obama's communications director, stating the White House line. "There is no small tactical shift we could have made at any point that would have solved that problem."

But while this explanation might be valid, it was also incomplete. A sense of disappointment, bordering on

Home alone *The President takes in a quiet moment in the Oval Office in June*

betrayal, had been growing across the country, especially in moderate states like Indiana. The fear most often expressed was that Obama was taking Americans somewhere they don't want to go. "We bought what he said. He offered a lot of hope," said Fred Ferlic, an Obama voter and orthopedic surgeon in South Bend who has since soured on his choice. Ferlic talked about the messy compromises in health-care reform, his sense of an inhospitable climate for businesses and the growth of government spending under Obama. "He's trying to Europeanize us, and the Europeans are going the other way," continued Ferlic, a former Democratic campaign donor.

One explanation for Obama's steep decline is that his presidency rests on what Gallup's Frank Newport calls a "paradox" between Obama and the electorate. In 2008, Newport notes, trust in the Federal Government was at a historic low, having dropped to around 25%, where it still remains. Yet Obama offered government as the primary solution to most of the nation's woes, calling for major new investments in health care, education, infrastructure and energy. Some voters bucked at the incongruity, repeatedly telling pollsters that even programs that have clearly helped the economy, like the $787 billion stimulus, did no such thing. Meanwhile, the resulting spike in deficits, which has been greatly magnified by tax revenue lost to the economic downturn, spooked a broad sweep of the country, which does not trust Washington to responsibly handle such a massive liability.

Rather than address these concerns as the economic crisis grew, Obama made a conscious choice to go big with government reforms of health care and energy. The bailouts of the auto companies, the rescue of Wall Street and the new regulation of banks and the rest of the financial industry only deepened the public's skepticism, especially among independent voters. Rather than dwell on the political problems, the President pushed his team forward, believing, in the words of top adviser David Axelrod, that "ultimately the best politics was to do that which he thought was right."

Yet even as Obama aides were aware of a growing disconnect, it didn't seem to worry their boss. Instead, the ambitious legislative goals usually trumped other priorities. Both in the original stimulus package and then in the health care and energy measures, the White House ceded most of its clout to the liberal lions who controlled the Democratic majorities in the House and Senate. That maneuver helped ensure passage of reforms, but it also confirmed some of the worst fears about how Washington works. "I'd rather be a one-term President and do big things than a two-term President and just do small things," he told his team after some in the Administration suggested pulling back on health-care reform.

In addition, for someone who so carefully read and responded to the political mood as a candidate, Obama was unexpectedly passive at moments as President. Whereas other Democrats had hoped to spend the late summer talking about two things—jobs and the unpopularity of many Republican proposals—the White House was dis-

Rewiring U.S. Society. Obama's two major legislative victories

HEALTH-CARE REFORM
On March 23, 2010, President Obama signed into law the Patient Protection and Affordable Care Act, the largest reform of U.S. health care since the 1960s. The bill passed the Senate on Dec. 24, 2009, by a vote of 60 to 39, and it was passed by the House on March 21, 2010, by a vote of 219 to 212. No Republican in either chamber voted for the bill; many in the GOP denounced it as a government takeover of health care. In broad outline, the bill seeks to reduce the number of Americans who lack health insurance by 32 million and reduce insurance company abuses and the federal deficit. Polls showed that while most Americans agreed with many individual provisions, they opposed the full bill. In August, Health and Human Services Secretary Kathleen Sebelius said the Administration had "a lot of re-education to do."

FINANCE REFORM
President Obama signed the Dodd-Frank Wall Street Reform and Consumer Protection Act into law on July 21, 2010. The law will institute sweeping reforms intended to address the practices that led to the Wall Street financial meltdown of 2007-08. It creates new federal regulatory agencies to oversee financial transactions and ensure more transparency in financial instruments. It also will create a new federal agency to protect consumers and investors. Like health-care reform, the bill passed in Congress along party lines; however, G.O.P. Senator Scott Brown of Massachusetts voted for the bill, saying, "It's not perfect, but it does a lot of positive things."

tracted by a string of unrelated issues, from immigration reform to a mishandled dismissal of a longtime USDA official to the furor over the proposed Islamic cultural center and mosque near Ground Zero. "It is inconceivable that a team so disciplined during the presidential campaign can't carry a message with the bully pulpit of the White House," said a Democratic strategist working on the midterm elections. "It's politically irresponsible, and Americans have little patience for it."

As his poll numbers fell, Obama responded with his perpetual cool. He acted less like an action-oriented President than a Prime Minister overseeing some vast but balky legislative machinery. When challenged about his declining popularity, the President tended to deflect the blame—to the state of the economy, the ferocity of the news cycle and right-wing misinformation campaigns. Aides treated the problem as a communications concern more than a matter of policy. They increased his travel schedule to key states and limited his prime-time addresses. They struggled to explain large, unpopular legislative packages to Americans who opposed the measures despite supporting many of their component parts, like extending health insurance to patients with pre-existing conditions or preventing teacher layoffs.

Instead of shifting course, Obama spoke dismissively about Republican efforts to play "short-term politics." He continued the near weekly visits to new green energy manufacturing plants, repeating promises of an economic rebirth that remains, for many, months or years away. By the end of the summer, the disconnect had grown so severe that only 1 in 3 Americans in a Pew poll accurately identified him as a Christian, down from 51% in October 2008. At the same time, the base voters Obama had energized so well in 2008 went back into hibernation, many of them suffering from the economic slump.

As the election approached, there was a growing belief in Washington that the Republicans would win the House in November and, if their stars aligned, have a good shot at taking the Senate as well. That sweep didn't happen, but when Republicans took the House and substantially reduced the Democrats' majority in the Senate, it was clear that Obama's brief window of one-party rule had closed. That outcome alone may justify Obama's decision to pursue the massive reforms while he still had the votes. It will never be known for certain just how much a more centrist legislative strategy would have improved the Democrats' midterm outlook.

Obama's aides continue to argue that the Administration's controversial reforms in health care and financial rules will produce benefits that voters will feel by 2012—benefits that escaped them in 2010. That would vindicate the President's vision of government as a solution and not just a problem. Even in Indiana, the disappointment in Obama was matched by a real yearning for a leader who can make a difference. "I think he's trying," Griffin, the laid-off payroll administrator who said she didn't know what Obama had done for her, told TIME's Scherer. "Nobody can turn it around overnight." ■

All the President's Men. Obama's staff gets a shake-up

RAHM EMANUEL
The profane, colorful White House chief of staff, 50, left to run for the job he always claimed he most desired, mayor of Chicago, after longtime mayor Richard M. Daley surprised just about everyone when he announced on Sept. 7 that he would not seek re-election. Emanuel resigned within the month, and Obama aide Pete Rouse took over on an interim basis.

LAWRENCE SUMMERS
Obama's outspoken head of the National Economic Council was the top voice on economic policy within the Administration. On Sept. 21 the White House said the combative Summers, 55, would be leaving and would resume his career at Harvard University, where Summers served a highly controversial term as president from 2001 to 2006.

PETER ORSZAG
The economist, 41, served as Director of the Office of Management and Budget under Obama and played a key role in the economic and legislative battles that marked the President's first two years in office. When he left on July 30, Jeffery Zients took over as acting director.

"I'd rather be a one-term President and do big things than a two-term President and just do small things"

—BARACK OBAMA, TO AIDES

Calamity In the Gulf

A leaking oil well gushes for three months, fouling the Gulf of Mexico and staining a host of reputations

SOME DISASTERS, LIKE THE EARTHQUAKE THAT devastated Haiti in January 2010, strike quickly. But the catastrophe that took place in the Gulf of Mexico three months later turned out to be a slow-motion nightmare. From April 20, the day crude oil began spewing from energy giant British Petroleum's partially blown well thousands of feet below the surface of the Gulf, it was obvious that a major environmental disaster was unfolding. But no one imagined that the well would continue to leak, defying all attempts to halt its flow, for almost three months, until the wellhead was capped on July 15. As oil gushed from the well, its ceaseless flow damaged one of the great fisheries in the U.S., polluted Gulf waters, fouled the shoreline, dried up the region's vital tourism industry—and left Americans further frustrated over their reliance on Big Oil and their government's management of U.S. energy reserves.

The saga began when the Deepwater Horizon oil rig, located some 50 miles (80.5 km) off the Louisiana coast,

Firefight *Above, boats spray the burning Deepwater Horizon oil rig on April 21; at left, a protest rally in New Orleans*

exploded and sank, killing 11 roughnecks, injuring 17 more and forcing the evacuation of 98 others. The rig was owned by Transocean, the world's largest operator of such platforms, and was being leased by British Petroleum (BP). When it exploded, the riser pipe connecting it to the well bent and broke, falling 5,000 ft. (1.5 km) to the ocean floor, and the wellhead began leaking crude oil, a sign that the blowout preventer atop the wellhead had not kicked on. Attempts to use underwater robots to activate the preventer and seal the well also failed.

BP officials initially downplayed the extent of the leakage from the spill. On April 29, a week after the rig exploded, the company reported that oil was leaking from the burst well at a rate of 5,000 bbl. a day, five times faster than BP had first estimated. This new figure, in turn, would be shown to be very far from the truth.

Within days of the explosion, BP secured approval from the U.S. Interior Department to drill a relief well that would divert and collect the flow from the wellhead, but executives noted it would be months before

The spill that killed *At left, oil permeates a wave flowing onto the Alabama coast. At right, a dead drumfish washes ashore in Mississippi*

it was ready. In the weeks to come, the company would mount a number of attempts to cap the undersea gusher, to no avail. Meanwhile, with each passing day, concerns grew over the future of the Gulf Coast's $2.4 billion fishing industry, as well as its lucrative tourism industries.

The crisis threatened the economic vitality of a region still recovering from the devastation wrought by Hurricane Katrina in 2005. And as with Katrina, it put the U.S. government on the spot. The Obama Administration could do little to plug the leaking wellhead, although as the days ticked by, calls rose for the government to take control of the containment effort. But, as TIME's Jeffrey Kluger pointed out in May, "the problem is, the ultimate solution to the disaster—stopping the gusher—has to be performed on the ocean floor. It's industry that does this kind of thing for a living, and it's industry that has the submersibles, the know-how and the trained personnel at the ready. The fact that BP hasn't succeeded yet does not mean that there's anyone better out there."

There was no doubt, however, as to who would pay for the enormous expense involved in cleaning up the Gulf waters, restoring the coast and reimbursing local businesses for their lost income. The Oil Pollution Act of 1990, passed in the wake of the *Exxon Valdez* disaster, explicitly places the burden of cleaning up a spill on the company that caused it but vests the President with the authority to mobilize federal or state assets to ensure the work gets done. The Coast Guard—perhaps the only federal agency that distinguished itself during the Hurri-

cane Katrina disaster—had been on the scene in the Gulf almost since the beginning of the emergency, helping supervise the more than 1,000 vessels and 22,000 people who had been at work trying to contain, burn and disperse the oil in the first days after the spill.

On May 1, President Obama appointed Coast Guard Admiral Thad Allen, a respected, experienced officer, as the Federal Government's top representative in the Gulf crisis. The next day, Obama visited the stricken region for the first time and hammered home the message the White House wanted Americans to hear. "Let me be clear," Obama declared, standing on the beach in the coastal fishing town of Venice, La., "BP is responsible for this leak. BP will be paying the bill."

A Desperate Fight to Save the Gulf

As the President spoke, frantic efforts continued on two fronts: to plug the leaking well and to collect the gushing crude. By early May, a flotilla of vessels had sprayed more than 140,000 gal. (530,000 l) of chemical dispersants on the oil slick, which by then had reached the size of Puerto Rico and was still growing. And responders had arrayed nearly 300,000 ft. (91,440 m) of floating booms to corral and concentrate the oil, allowing it to be skimmed off the surface. Nature wasn't helping: high winds made it harder for many responders, especially local fishermen operating smaller craft, to navigate the rocky waters.

On May 2, the day Obama visited Louisiana, the National Oceanic and Atmospheric Administration (NOAA)

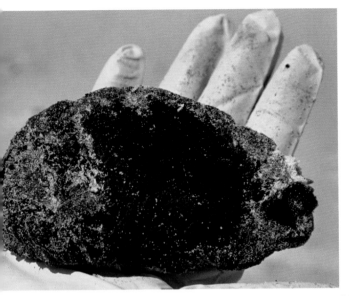

One big mess *On left, a tar ball that was found in Alabama; at right, marine biologists examine oil near Venice, La.*

closed fishing for 10 days from points east of the mouth of the Mississippi River to the waters just off the Florida Panhandle, a region that produces a significant portion of North America's fish, crabs, oysters and shrimp.

Local fishermen joined a growing chorus of voices around the nation in blasting BP's response to the crisis. "The oil people behind them desks, they don't know what they did, and they don't know the bayou," Venice fisherman Billy De La Cruz told TIME. Two weeks later, BP CEO Tony Hayward, whose response to the crisis was surprisingly tone-deaf, proved De La Cruz right, telling Britain's Sky News that he didn't think the spill would seriously hurt the Gulf ecosystem. "Everything we can see at the moment suggests that the overall environmental impact will be very, very modest," he opined.

Hayward's claims were met with shock and derision, for by now independent scientists had found that BP had radically low-balled its estimate of the extent of the leak, claiming the well was discharging roughly 5,000 bbl., or 210,000 gal., of oil a day. But scientists studying a video feed of the gusher and measuring the growing slick at the surface suggested it could be five to 16 times that rate (the final estimate was 53,000 to 62,000 bbl. a day).

The revelations that the leak was far more severe than previously claimed intensified Americans' concerns over the impact of the spill. Consumers mounted boycotts of BP, a company that had invested heavily in promoting itself as an advocate of a greener energy future. Republicans, whose presidential campaign rallies in 2008

The Spill by the Numbers.
The dismal statistics of a man-made disaster

86 days

The length of time it took to cap British Petroleum's undersea wellhead following the explosion and sinking of the Deepwater Horizon drill rig on April 20. Inquiries are ongoing, but BP has admitted that a series of errors aboard the rig triggered the disaster.

53,000

The number of barrels of heavy crude oil leaking each day from the well when it was finally capped on July 15, down from its most excessive rate of flow, when it was leaking 62,000 bbl. each day. In the first days after the spill, BP executives said the well was leaking only some 5,000 bbl. a day.

10 miles

The length of one large oil plume found beneath the sea by U.S. scientists. On May 30, scientists from the University of South Florida reported measuring huge toxic clouds of oil moving deep beneath the surface. Three days later, BP CEO Tony Hayward said, "The oil is on the surface. There aren't any plumes."

had featured thousands of voices chanting "Drill, baby, drill," focused on attacking the White House response to the crisis as fitful and inept. Surprisingly, the Administration found itself on the wrong side of the drilling issue: only four weeks before the crisis began, President Obama had called for the resumption of some offshore drilling, an overture designed to win a few GOP votes in Congress for climate-change legislation. Now the White House dialed back its position, and Obama ordered a six-month moratorium on all offshore drilling. When the order was overturned by a federal appeals court in New Orleans, the Administration put in place a slightly modified moratorium on drilling.

Nor could the Administration paper over the charge that lax federal oversight had helped allow the problem to occur in the first place. Enforcing safety rules is the responsibility of the Interior Department's Minerals Management Service. A May 25 article in the New York *Times* reported on MMS misconduct from 2005 to 2008, including bribery of inspectors who accepted meals, tickets to sporting events and other gifts from well owners whose projects they were overseeing; one inspector was reportedly under the influence of crystal meth during an on-site inspection. In addition, MMS staffers allowed oil companies to fill out their own inspection reports in pencil, which were then committed to ink

Residue of a disaster
At left, Kaan Ciftci waits for diners to arrive at the Boardwalk Cafe in Pensacola, Fla., in June. The region's tourism industry was slammed by the spill.

Below, a shrimp boat collects crude oil floating on the surface of the Gulf in large skimmer nets

by MMS regulators. Those were Bush-era incidents, but the MMS was under Obama's control in 2010, and it fell to his White House to put its affairs in order. "We need to clean house," Interior Secretary Ken Salazar told the Senate Energy and Natural Resources Committee. Meanwhile, U.S. Attorney General Eric Holder announced on June 1 that the Federal Government would launch investigations into the spill to trace its original causes. "If we find evidence of illegal behavior, we will be extremely forceful in our response," Holder said.

The Leak is Sealed, But the Stain Remains

By late May, tar balls—the solidified residue of the leaked crude—were washing up on Florida shores, and NOAA had expanded the no-fishing zone; nearly one-fifth of the Gulf, more than 47,000 sq. mi., (122,00 sq. km.) was now off-limits for fishing. Back at the wellhead, attention focused on BP's latest attempt to stanch the leak, a method known as "top-kill," which involved pumping a heavy, mudlike substance into the broken well pipe to stop the flow, then sealing it with concrete. For more than a week, BP promised that the top-kill attempt was just a day or two away, but the schedule slipped repeatedly, despite the company's official optimism. "We rate the probability of success between 60% and 70%," declared CEO Hayward. Days later, on May 29, the top-kill method failed. A few weeks later, a similarly ballyhooed attempt to place a containment dome over the well also failed.

The crisis continued through June and into July, as more and more federal fishing waters were placed off-limits and the Gulf's summer tourism industry took a severe hit. At last, on July 15, BP managed to put in place a cap that stopped the leak. The relief well that diverted the oil flow went online on Sept. 16. Finally, on Sept. 19, Allen declared the well "effectively dead." That was good news, but the full impact of the accident won't be evident for years, although a consensus seemed to be growing that the effects of the spill may turn out to be less damaging than some had warned during the initial panic over the accident. But the spill's effect on a restless American public was already clear: the worst environmental crisis in U.S. history had stained not just the Gulf's waters but seemingly everyone it touched. ∎

"Everything we can see at the moment suggests that the overall environmental impact will be very, very modest"

—BP CEO TONY HAYWARD

In the Hot Seat. Portraits in damage control

Tony Hayward
The British CEO's response to the oil spill will be studied for decades in business schools—as an example of how not to manage a crisis. His string of gaffes included remarking that "there's no one who wants this thing over more than I do. I'd like my life back." After he stonewalled a House committee investigating the incident, he was finally dismissed by the BP board on July 27.

Thad Allen
As national incident commander for the disaster, the Admiral, who retired from the Coast Guard on June 30, was the point man for the government's response to the spill. His candor and competence—honed when he took over rescue operations from a fumbling FEMA during the Hurricane Katrina crisis in 2005—brought an aura of calm to the Gulf catastrophe.

Barack Obama
Determined not to allow the spill to become "Obama's Katrina," the President visited the Gulf four times before the leak was capped. Accused of hesitation in an interview on NBC's *Today Show,* he replied: "I don't sit around just talking to experts because this is a college seminar. We talk to these folks because they potentially have the best answer, so I know whose ass to kick."

Robert Gates

With straight talk and swift deeds, the Secretary of Defense
has earned the respect of both politicians and the Pentagon

SECRETARY OF DEFENSE ROBERT GATES FLIES
around the world to war zones and allies, to
China and Russia and Suriname, on a cold
war relic called the *Doomsday Plane*. Forged in the
1970s by Boeing, it was designed to stay aloft even
in the midst of nuclear war. It's an airborne Pentagon.
The plane is so heavy that it needs refueling in midair
on long flights. It's one of a handful of planes coated
with nuclear-radiation shielding and capable of emit-
ting launch codes to all U.S. missile silos.

Like his fellow cold war survivor the *Doomsday Plane*,
Gates has come to embody power, control and an astonishing longevity. Just 5 ft. 8 in., with small hands and
feet, the demure 67-year-old Kansan has outlasted seven
Presidents as well as most of his fellow bureaucrats and
policymakers. He's the only entry-level CIA analyst to
rise to the top job, Director of Central Intelligence. And
he's the only Secretary of Defense ever to be asked to
stay on in a rival party's Administration. He has thrived
through a combination of endurance, pragmatism and
bureaucratic savvy. And on issue after issue —Pentagon
reform, missile defense, Afghanistan and the Pentagon's
move to repeal the "Don't ask, don't tell" policy on gays
in the military—Gates has become the most important
player in the Obama war cabinet. It's a remarkable feat,
considering that he's the only Republican on the Democratic national-security team.

Gates is a careful, restrained player who wields his
power with quiet but ruthless efficiency—as he did on
Feb. 1, 2010, when he fired the military officer overseeing the Pentagon's new F-35 stealth-fighter-jet program
for cost overruns and technical failures and punished
Lockheed Martin by withholding $615 million in fees.
Lots of defense contractors and program managers
underachieve, yet they almost always get away with it.
Not under Gates.

In December 2009, Gates won passage of a watershed
Pentagon budget that shifted spending from theoreti-
cal, conventional wars to the unconventional ones
the military is actually fighting now. Months later,
Gates helped Obama execute a surge in Afghanistan,
a plan the President had campaigned on in 2008 but
which has since become known as the "Gates option."

"Sixty-two thousand forces committed in one year of a
liberal Democratic President's first term? That's pretty
remarkable," a senior Defense official told TIME's
Elizabeth Rubin.

A consummate technocrat, Gates is a comforting
presence who puts a face on the predictability of
uncertainty. His Wichita monotone and old-fashioned
speeches about service and duty exude a sense of calm
and control—just what the Pentagon needed at the
end of 2006 as an antidote to the departing Donald
Rumsfeld. Gates had left the CIA in 1993 and become
president of Texas A&M University before being called
back to Washington by George W. Bush. At Gates'
confirmation hearings, Democratic Senator Carl Levin
asked whether the U.S. was winning the war in Iraq.
Gates replied, "No, sir." With those two words, he won
over the Democrats in the bitterly divided Congress.
(He also said he didn't think the U.S. was losing.)

Gates walked into the Pentagon alone. Inheriting
many former Rumsfeld aides, Gates told them on his
first day that he wouldn't be firing anyone. There was
no time for confirmations, and he was leaving that
day for Iraq. Gates brought a sense of relief, a feeling
that an adult was back in charge. Two months into
his tenure, the Washington *Post* broke the scandal
about the miserable conditions at Walter Reed Army
Medical Center and the outdated bureaucracy faced
by wounded soldiers just to get medical attention and
benefits. Gates fired the Army's secretary and surgeon
general and the hospital commander. The special-ops
community nicknamed him the Black Chinook—he
lands at night, takes care of business and gets out. He
might approve: at least the Chinook is more up-to-date
and efficient than the *Doomsday Plane*. ∎

**The special-ops community
nicknamed Secretary Gates
the Black Chinook—he
lands at night, takes care
of business and gets out.**

Obama's man at the Pentagon *Gates studies a memo aboard the* Doomsday Plane *in August 2010. The Secretary of Defense has the President's full confidence, but he has warned that he may leave his post before 2012*

In Arizona, A War Over The Border

State legislators pass a tough new law against illegal immigration, but opponents say it promotes racial profiling and violates civil liberties

AMERICA'S BATTLES OVER ILLEGAL IMMIGRATION from south of the border had been simmering at a low boil since the last years of the Bush Administration. But in 2010 all the old passions came roaring back to life when SB1070, the toughest anti-illegal-immigrant measure in a generation, was passed by the Arizona legislature on April 19 and quickly signed into law by Republican Governor Jan Brewer, 66, a strong supporter. The law gave local police sweeping new powers in regard to undocumented workers. Before its passage, immigration offenses were violations of federal, not state, law. Under SB1070, however, Arizona police would have the right to question anyone they stopped on "reasonable suspicion" that he or she might be an illegal immigrant and could arrest those who weren't carrying a valid driver's license or identity papers.

Feelings on the subject run high in Arizona, a point of entry for thousands of undocumented workers going to the U.S. from Mexico, and tensions were heightened by the early-2010 murder of a rancher in a remote border area where illegal crossings are rampant. With 6.6 million residents, Arizona is estimated to have half a million illegal immigrants. Small wonder that both proponents

and opponents of the law were vociferous. "The bill constitutes a complete disregard for the rights of nonwhites in Arizona. It effectively mandates racial profiling," said Chris Newman, legal director of the National Day Laborer Organizing Network, expressing widespread concerns that local police could stop Hispanics for minor offenses as a pretext for questioning their immigration status. But state senator Russell Pearce, a Republican, said his bill "will not change a thing for lawful citizens. It simply takes the handcuffs off law enforcement and allows them to do their job. Our legal citizens have a constitutional right to expect protection of federal law against noncitizens. When those laws are not enforced, our citizens are denied equal protection."

The legislation sparked intense debate across the nation. Large rallies supporting and opposing the law were held, and its opponents called for consumer boycotts of Arizona tourism and conventions. Phil Gordon, the mayor of Phoenix, called SB1070 a "hateful law." President Barack Obama took the unusual step of commenting on a state statute, calling SB1070 "misguided" and ordering the Justice Department to look into the legislation. Some experts claimed that under Article 1 of the Constitution,

Divided nations *At left is a portion of the U.S.-built barrier between Arizona, right, and Mexico, on left, outside Naco, Ariz.*

Divided state *The new law's foes, like the protesters above at a Phoenix rally, said it discriminated against Hispanic Americans. But Governor Brewer, right, supported the law*

only Congress has the power to create immigration law.

As for the border crime and cartel violence that have fueled much of Arizona's anxiety about immigration, there's little in SB1070 that would directly address them. "The tea baggers and company aren't the only ones who are frustrated. We need more border patrol," said Attorney General Terry Goddard, who was running for governor as a Democrat. "But the serious crime is the human smugglers, the dope smugglers. [SB1070] doesn't do one thing to fight that."

But the bill found millions of ardent supporters in Arizona and across the nation. J.D. Hayworth, a former Representative seeking a U.S. Senate seat who was later

> ## "The serious crime is the human smugglers, the dope smugglers. [Arizona's new immigration law] doesn't do one thing to fight that."
> —ARIZONA ATTORNEY GENERAL TERRY GODDARD

beaten by Senator John McCain in the Republican primary, said, "When the Federal Government failed to act, Arizonans did. [Arizonans] have been asking for years to have the Federal Government secure that border." Largely because of that frustration, polls showed that a wide majority of Arizona's voters backed SB1070, while a number of national polls showed about 50% of Americans favored the law and 40% opposed it. By August, legislatures in 17 states had introduced bills modeled on it.

On July 6, the Justice Department filed suit in a federal court to block implementation of the law, and on July 28, U.S. District Judge Susan R. Bolton blocked the most contentious portions of the statute only a day before they were scheduled to take effect. Agreeing with the Justice Department that the law intruded into federal immigration enforcement, Bolton put on hold its provisions that would require police to check the immigration status of those stopped for any kind of questioning, would allow the arrest without warrant of suspected illegal immigrants and would criminalize immigrants who failed to carry registration papers. The ruling set up a battle that will take place quite a ways from the Arizona border: in the U.S. Supreme Court. ∎

Academic ties *President Obama announces Kagan's nomination: the two share links with Harvard and the University of Chicago*

Elena Kagan

The U.S. Solicitor General and former dean of the Harvard Law School joins two other women on the Supreme Court

O N MONDAY, MAY 10, 2010, PRESIDENT BARACK Obama strode to a microphone in the East Room of the White House to announce his nominee to replace long-serving Supreme Court Justice John Paul Stevens, due to retire from the court at 90 on June 28. Obama's choice was no surprise: it was U.S. Solicitor General Elena Kagan, 50, former dean of the Harvard Law School. "Elena is respected and admired, not just for her intellect and record of achievement," the President declared, "but also for her temperament, her openness to a broad array of view-points, her habit—to borrow a phrase from Justice Stevens—of understanding before disagreeing, her fair-mindedness and skill as a consensus builder."

During the selection process, Obama reviewed the writings of two dozen potential Justices; he and Vice President Joe Biden spoke with four candidates privately, including both Kagan and Seventh Circuit Judge Diane Wood, who were both finalists in 2009 for the open seat that went to Sonia Sotomayor. Obama, reported an aide, had heard from several Senators about a desire to find someone, like Kagan, who had not already served as a judge.

Raised on the Upper West Side of Manhattan, Kagan boasted a résumé that uncannily resembled that of the rest of the members of the highest court:

a graduate of the Ivy League, schooled at Princeton and Harvard Law School. She clerked for Supreme Court Justice Thurgood Marshall and D.C. Circuit Judge Abner Mikva, who is one of Obama's Chicago mentors. Kagan taught at the University of Chicago in the early 1990s, where she first met Obama.

Kagan was well known on Capitol Hill. She served for much of President Clinton's second term as a domestic policy adviser in the White House, where she was regarded as a pragmatic problem-solver with centrist views. In 1999, she was nominated by Clinton to the D.C. Circuit, but Senate Republicans blocked a hearing and vote on her nomination.

Despite the deep and divisive ideological rifts between the Senate's Republicans and Democrats, Kagan sailed through her confirmation hearings before the Senate Judiciary Committee with only minor scratches. The most prominent flash point on her record involved her decision in 2004 to ban military recruitment on the Harvard Law School campus while a case involving federal funding for schools that forbade such efforts went to the Supreme Court. Kagan had cited the military's "Don't Ask, Don't Tell" policy as the reason for the ban. In 2005 the Federal Government threatened to withhold all funding from the school, and Kagan reversed herself, reopening the school to recruiters. But although

several Republican Senators attacked Kagan's actions, the issue failed to gain traction. One Republican, Senator Lindsey Graham of South Carolina, joined Democrats in voting for Kagan, as the committee approved her nomination by a 13-to-6 vote.

The full Senate approved Kagan's nomination on Aug. 5 by a vote of 63 to 37, with five Republicans voting for her and one Democrat against. Two days later, she was sworn in by Chief Justice John Roberts, becoming the fourth female Justice in the history of the Supreme Court, the eighth Jewish Justice to sit on the court and the first nominee since 1972 with no prior experience as a judge. Kagan will also be the youngest judge on the court, prompting TV satirist Stephen Colbert to declare, "She's just a kid. And she's going to be distracting all of the other Justices with her squealing over Justin Bieber." ∎

"She would not have been someone I would have chosen, but the person who did choose, President Obama, chose wisely."

—SENATOR LINDSEY GRAHAM

Not-so-hot seat *Kagan seemed to charm members of the Senate Judiciary Committee, often drawing laughter with her quick wit*

Close call *Surveillance-camera footage shows a vehicle, packed with explosives, passing through the crowded Broadway theater district in New York City*

A Scare in Times Square

Alert street vendors work with police and foil an amateurish—but potentially deadly—bombing in one of the busiest areas of the U.S.

ASSUMING YOU WANTED TO DO A LOT OF DAMAGE with a well-rigged car bomb, the junction of West 45th Street and Broadway in midtown Manhattan, where Times Square narrows into an asphalt bottleneck, would be the place to pick. If the bomb planted in a green 1993 Nissan Pathfinder SUV on the evening of May 1 had exploded, here's what would have happened, according to retired New York police department bomb-squad detective Kevin Barry. The car would have turned into a "boiling liquid explosive." The propane tanks that fueled the bomb would have overheated and ignited into "huge blowtorches" that could have been ejected from the vehicle. The explosion, lasting only a few seconds, would have created a thermal ball wide enough to

swallow up most of the intersection. A blast wave would have rocketed out in all directions; hitting the surrounding buildings, the wave would have bounced off and kept going, as much as nine times as fast as before. Anyone standing within 1,400 ft. (430 m)—about five city blocks—of the explosion would have been at risk of being hit by shrapnel and millions of shards of flying glass.

Such horrors did not come to New York for what you might call a New York reason. Amid all the bumping and crowding and hustling that make Times Square what it is hides a resident network of people who watch one another's backs. On one corner, Lance Orton sells T shirts at his stall; across the street is fellow Vietnam vet Duane Jackson, a handbag and scarf vendor. Rallis Gialaboukis

Shahzad *The would-be bomber lived in Bridgeport, Ct., and became a U.S. citizen in April 2009. That summer he traveled to Pakistan, where he reportedly received training in terror tactics*

has his hot-dog cart next to Jackson. And then there's Bullet, the homeless guy who darts from stall to stall, chatting everyone up. Their collective alarms went off when smoke started coming out of the Pathfinder, left with its engine running in front of a phone booth, already conspicuous because it was illegally parked in a bus lane. The cops were called in; the area was evacuated. And the city that never sleeps had one more reason to thank its street-level watchdogs who always seem to stay wide awake.

Less than 54 hours after the police were alerted, a suspect was taken into custody. Authorities traced Faisal Shahzad, 30, a naturalized U.S. citizen from Pakistan, through his SUV's vehicle identification number. Even so, he almost fled the country. After authorities on his tail lost track of him, he was arrested on a plane at John F. Kennedy airport that was sitting on the runway, preparing to depart for Dubai. Authorities later said Shahzad had confessed to receiving bombmaking training in Waziristan, part of Pakistan's tribal regions along its frontier border with Afghanistan. He also claimed to have been in contact with the Yemen-based, American-born jihad proponent Anwar al-Awlaki.

After Shahzad's arrest, many Americans chose to mock the amateurish nature of the bomb attempt. A gun locker inside the SUV, for example, contained fertilizer that was incapable of exploding. But skill is one thing, intentions another. The bomb in Times Square was not the work of some addle-brained nut job, acting alone. It was terrorism, planned in collaboration with international jihadists: an attempt, for political reasons, to kill Americans. Lots of them. That's the bad news. The good news: alert Americans took action and thwarted the attack. On June 21, Faisal Shahzad pleaded guilty to 10 counts of terrorism-related charges, including attempting to use a weapon of mass destruction. As of November 2010, he was being held in a New York City jail, and he is expected to serve a mandatory life term in prison. ∎

Airborne Terrorism.
A Christmas attack is thwarted

The last week of 2009 saw an airline terrorist attack fail, as 23-year-old Umar Farouk Abdulmutallab, a Nigerian citizen, was tackled by a Dutch passenger aboard Northwest Airlines Flight 253, bound from Amsterdam to Detroit, when Abdulmutallab attempted to set off plastic explosives concealed in his underwear. They failed to detonate properly, resulting in flames and popping noises. Abdulmutallab was indicted on two counts of terrorism-related charges and was awaiting trial as of November 2010; if convicted, he could serve a mandatory life term.

The son of a wealthy banker, Abdulmutallab is believed to have been influenced by Anwar al-Awlaki, the same prophet of terrorism who influenced would-be Times Square bomber Faisal Shahzad. In the wake of the failed airline bombing, President Barack Obama strongly criticized U.S. intelligence agencies, whom he described as having enough information about Abdulmutallab's intentions to deny him the opportunity to board a plane bound for the U.S.

In Brief

Disasters

VENICE IN TENNESSEE *"That is an astonishing amount of rain in a 24- or 36-hour period,"* *said Tennessee Governor Phil Bredesen, after more than 13 inches of rain fell in Nashville* *over two days in May, sending the waters of the Cumberland River coursing through* *Music City, above. Twenty-one deaths were blamed on the flood in Tennessee, while six* *died in northern Mississippi and four in Kentucky, also hard-hit by the deluge.*

Society

Is America Islamophoic?

That question was put to readers on the cover of TIME's Aug. 30 issue, as anti-Islamic incidents around the nation multiplied. The noisiest uproar, fanned by right-leaning commentators, erupted over plans to build a Muslim cultural center and mosque two blocks from Ground Zero in Manhattan. Critics charged the center would offend the families of 9/11 victims and would taint an area widely regarded as sacred. The facts that the building was not on the Ground Zero site and that local Muslims had already been praying in the building for nearly a year were lost amid the furor, as protests peaked in August.

As the anti-Islamic tide rose, Florida fundamentalist Christian pastor Rev. Terry Jones declared he would conduct a burning of the Koran at his church on Sept. 11. He was eventually dissuaded, having gained national attention: mission accomplished. A late-summer TIME/Abt SRBI poll found that 61% of Americans opposed the Park51 project, with just 26% in favor of it. And almost 25% believed the false charge that President Barack Obama is a Muslim.

Extremists

A Rise in Right-Wing Militias

As political rhetoric reached new extremes in the U.S. in 2010, a TIME report by Pulitzer prizewinning investigative correspondent Barton Gellman explored the world of antigoverment alienation and documented the advent of a new generation of right-wing militias around the nation. Below, members of one such group, the Ohio Defense Force, take part in practice maneuvers in August.

Gellman's six-month investigation

revealed that among such extreme groups, recruiting, planning, training and explicit calls for a shooting war were rising steeply, as were criminal investigations by the FBI and state authorities.

National Security
Spy vs. Spy: It's Back

Remember the cold war? It returned with a splash at the end of June, when the FBI said it had arrested 10 "deep-cover agents" planted in the U.S. by the Russian Federation; another was identified in Cyprus. On July 9, the 10 spies in the U.S., all of whom pleaded guilty to conspiracy charges, were flown to Vienna and exchanged for four Russian nationals accused of working for western spy agencies. Below, a sketch of some of the spies.

Cities
Chicago's Daley: Farewell

Richard M. Daley spent 21 years as Chicago's mayor before announcing on Sept. 7 that he would not seek re-election. His father Richard J. Daley also spent 21 years in the same job; together, they leave a mighty urban legacy. Although tough and sometimes imperious like his dad, the son had a more ambitious vision, guiding Chicago into a cosmopolitan future through support for the arts and development projects like the grand Millennium Park.

Disasters
Tragedy in West Virginia

Above, mining families mourn their loved ones following an April 5 explosion in the Upper Big Branch Mine in West Virginia that killed 29 men, making it the deadliest mining disaster in the U.S. in decades.

In the wake of the tragedy, records showed that mine operator Massey Energy had been cited by federal regulators with 1,324 safety violations in the past five years, many of them involving improper ventilation or inadequate escape routes.

The cause of the explosion is not yet known; it may involve a buildup of methane gas, which can be alleviated through proper ventilation. Despite the number of citations, the mine continued to operate, raising questions about the quality of government supervision and Massey's commitment to safety. Federal investigations are in progress.

Politics
Under the Microscope

Two veteran members of Congress and the former governors of two of the nation's largest states were in the news in 2010, amid polls showing the public's trust in government was at a low point.

ELIOT SPITZER

The former governor of New York, 51, once a fast-rising star of the Democratic Party, resigned in March 2008 after he was revealed to be a client of an upscale prostitution ring. He returned to the spotlight in 2010, debuting in October as co-host of a CNN political discussion program with newspaper columnist Kathleen Parker.

MAXINE WATERS

Now 72, Waters has served since 1991 as a Representative from California and is

the most senior of 12 black women in the House. In 2010 she was accused by a House subcommittee of ethics violations stemming from her husband's involvement with a Massachusetts bank. A trial is expected to begin late in 2010.

ROD BLAGOJEVICH

The former Illinois governor, 53, was impeached and removed from office early in 2009 following his arrest on federal corruption charges late in 2008. On Aug. 17, 2010, Blagojevich was convicted on one charge of lying to federal investigators; the jury was unable to reach a verdict on 23 other charges. A mistrial was declared, and federal prosecutors said they would bring Blagojevich to trial again.

CHARLES RANGEL

The Democratic Representative from New York City has served in the House since 1970; he

is now 80. On Nov. 16, after a two-day hearing, a House subcommittee found him guilty of 11 counts of ethics violations. He is not likely to be expelled from the chamber.

World

A Nation Mourns

Poland endured a national tragedy in 2010, when a Polish Air Force Tu-154 jet carrying many of the nation's leaders, including President Lech Kaczynski and his wife Maria, crashed in thick fog outside Smolensk, Russia, killing all 96 people aboard.

The delegation was traveling to meet with Russian leaders to observe the 70th anniversary of the Katyn massacre of 1940, in which Soviet secret police murdered some 22,000 Polish nationals, then blamed the crimes on the Nazis. The Soviet Union denied responsibility for the massacre until 1990, and the 2010 memorial service was intended to heal fissures between the two nations. At left, Girl Scouts light candles outside the presidential palace in Warsaw.

Tunnel Of Love

Trapped for 69 days, a group of 33 miners is rescued—and a watching world celebrates

BY THE TIME THE CAPSULE ROSE THROUGH THE mine shaft's manhole-size opening shortly after midnight, local time, on Oct. 13, the surrounding desert outside the northern Chilean city of Copiapó was as dark and cold as a sepulcher. But when 30-year-old Florencio Avalos emerged from 2,300 ft. (700 m) below the earth and into the arms of his wife and children, an incandescent fiesta of life erupted on the surrounding dunes and rock piles. The miner and 32 companions had been huddled in solitude since their gold and copper mine collapsed on Aug. 5; now the men who had been all but buried alive for 69 days were becoming the world's newest heroes.

The U.S. exulted in 1970 when it brought its three Apollo 13 astronauts back safely from a disaster in space. With the emergence of Avalos, Chile—and, for that matter, South America, a continent whose achievements are so often overshadowed by natural and political tragedy—celebrated its own finest hour as it rescued the 33 miners from the abyss. Chileans, not known for exuberance, unleashed deafening cheers and chants through the chilly air above the San José mine—"Tonight we bring them back!"—along with confetti and balloons bearing the Chilean flag. The sight of Avalos' 7-year-old son, wearing a hard hat and standing beside Chilean President Sebastián Piñera as he awaited his father, brought tears to many at Camp Hope, the rescue station set up at the mine.

"We made a promise to never surrender, and we kept it," said President Piñera, who arrived at the site, about

Unearthed *The Phoenix rescue capsule, hauled up from almost half a mile below the surface, emerges as rescue workers prepare to welcome a miner back from his ordeal*

49

Preparation *A video feed shows miners hugging Manuel Gonzalez, the first rescue worker to arrive at their refuge*

Exhilaration *Mario Gomez, the ninth of the 33 miners to emerge from the shaft, waves to the crowd as he exits the rescue capsule*

530 miles (850 km) north of Santiago, Chile's capital, the day before the rescue began. Earlier, he said that the miners' rescue would be "a true rebirth for us all." That rebirth, capping a survival record in the annals of mining disasters, became a prolonged celebration that transfixed a vast global audience. Indeed, the profound emotions generated by Operation San Lorenzo, named for the patron saint of miners, seemed to grow rather than diminish as each resurrected miner reached the surface.

The process of sending the 24-in. (61 cm) -wide capsule down the almost half-mile diagonal duct and then carrying each miner up to the surface initially took about an hour for each rescue, then sped up. It ended some 22 hours later, when the last of the miners emerged from the tunnel: Luis Urzúa, 52, the shift foreman who was the men's leader and kept them cohesive during their entrapment, a role he played throughout the rescue phase as well.

When Urzúa placed his foot on the ground, it brought

an end to an ordeal that began in early August, when the mine collapsed and the world feared the miners had been lost. But far below, the men were alive, gathered in a shelter measuring about 500 sq. ft. (45 sq m), no larger than a small studio apartment. With Urzúa in charge, they ate just two teaspoons of tuna and one biscuit every two days, washing down their "meals" with a small sip of milk. The meager rations helped keep them going for an incredible 17 days until the outside world learned the good news: against the odds, all 33 miners were still alive.

"*Estamos bien en el refugio, los 33,*" they wrote in a note attached to the end of a probe that bored into the shelter on Aug. 22. "We are well inside the shelter, the 33." Those first words came after several attempts to drill down and reach any surviving miners had failed. In those first moments after they were discovered, the men peered eagerly into a miniature camera, their eyes blazing with euphoria. Among their first requests: toothbrushes. Later, a second

69 Days
Buried Alive.
How the 33 survived: a timeline

AUG. 5
The shafts inside the gold and copper mine collapse in the early afternoon, leaving the group of 33 men trapped some 2,300 ft. (700 m) beneath the surface. Shift foreman Luis Urzúa takes charge of the survival operation.

AUG. 6 TO 22
Under Urzúa's leadership, the trapped miners subsist for 17 days on scant rations intended to last for only 48 hours. Meanwhile, on the surface, family members, Chileans and many others begin a long vigil, right, hoping the men are still alive.

Examination *Miner Juan Illanes is carried on a stretcher to a makeshift medical center at the rescue site, dubbed Camp Hope*

Jubilation *Chileans in downtown Copiapó cheer as the rescue begins. Thirty-two of the miners were Chilean; one was Bolivian*

bore hole was driven into the cavern; the 6-in. (15 cm) portal served as an umbilical cord delivering food, water, medicine and oxygen to the waiting men.

The final phase of the rescue operation began on Oct. 9, when a giant U.S.-operated drill finally bored a man-sized hole through the ceiling of the refuge, a good month before most rescue officials had expected. The men prepared for their ascent in the specially designed capsule, named Phoenix, by doing exercises assigned by doctors. On the trip, each wore a special helmet equipped with communications gear so officials could keep in constant contact with them; an oxygen mask and a belt with vital-signs sensors around the torso; and dark glasses to keep their eyes, more like those of moles now than of humans, from being damaged in the sudden return to light.

A problem with the capsule door delayed the operation's start, but Manuel Gonzalez, the first of a handful of rescue workers, was lowered down shortly after 11 p.m.

to gauge the miners' condition and assist them with the capsule. Within minutes Avalos, the No. 2 leader of the mining group, who had helped monitor his comrades' health for officials above, was on his way up. Each man was allowed to have about three family members greet him as he popped through the hole. He was examined by doctors at a makeshift medical facility at the rescue site, then whisked by helicopter to a hospital in Copiapó for a minimum of two days' observation.

As the joyous reunions continued, Margarita Rojo, 72, the mother of miner Dario Segovia, 48, admitted to Time that she had feared the rescue would not come so soon. Then again, she said, she was a miner herself as a younger woman, an explosives expert to boot. Her son, she said, "is a miner—they're like cats, with nine lives. He's got three or four left at least." For the two days of Operation San Lorenzo, that outpouring of life lit up the watching world as surely as it ignited the barren Chilean desert. ■

AUG. 22
A probe reaches the men's shelter, and they send back a handwritten note to say they are alive. Rescue operations had begun immediately, but due to inaccurate maps, a series of bore holes about 5 in. (12.7 cm) wide failed to locate the men.

AUG. 23 TO OCT. 9
Rescuers send down oxygen capsules, glucose and rehydration tablets to restore the men's digestive systems. Mario Sepúlveda, a.k.a. "Super Mario," begins sending video logs of the men's ordeal. The main drill breaks into the refuge on Oct. 9.

OCT. 13 AND 14
The miners begin emerging from the refuge, hauled up aboard the Phoenix capsule, which performed flawlessly; NASA engineers helped design it. The ascents each take about 15 minutes, and the rescue operation concludes after 22 hours.

In Search of A Turnaround

The war in Afghanistan grinds into its ninth year, with bad news outweighing good

ON FEB. 11, TWO DAYS BEFORE LAUNCHING THE most ambitious military campaign of the Obama Administration, General Stanley McChrystal, commander of U.S. and NATO forces in Afghanistan, convened a meeting in Kabul of 450 tribal elders and scholars from Helmand province. The general's objective: to build support for Operation Moshtarak, a massive offensive on the Taliban stronghold of Marjah. McChrystal ran through the military phase of the plan, which would involve 6,000 U.S. Marines and British soldiers and 4,500 Afghan troops and police. Then he described how these troops would protect the town while a "government in a box"—a corps of Afghan officials who had been training for this moment for months—would start administering the town. The elders all signed off on the plan, but not before one of them warned the American general, "You have to understand that if you don't do what you say, we'll all be killed."

McChrystal repeated the chieftain's words Feb. 18 in a secure video teleconference with President Barack Obama and his top advisers. By then, the operation, by all accounts, was going well. NATO troops had encountered only sporadic resistance; much of the town was under the control of the U.S. Marines. British-led forces, meanwhile, had taken the nearby community of Showal. Some government in a box was already being unpacked.

There was good news from other fronts as well early in the year. In Pakistan, a joint operation in Karachi by the CIA and Pakistan's spy agency, Inter-Services Intelligence (ISI), had netted a very big fish: Mullah Abdul Ghani Baradar, the Afghan Taliban's military chief. In quick succession, the ISI had also nabbed two of the Taliban's "shadow" governors of Afghanistan's provinces and another senior figure. And in North Waziristan, near Pakistan's border with Afghanistan, a missile launched

from a CIA drone had struck at the heart of the Haqqani Network, an al-Qaeda-affiliated group responsible for countless attacks on NATO troops. The network's current leader, Sirajuddin Haqqani, survived, but his younger brother Mohammed was killed.

Yet despite the rush of encouraging news, no one was celebrating, least of all in Obama's White House, as it sought to wind down U.S. involvement after nine years of a grinding war that polls showed fewer and fewer Americans supported. Sure enough: by the fall, the highly fluid situation looked completely different in many respects, although in its complexity it carried a familiar sense of déjà vu. The U.S., unexpectedly, had a new military commander in the theater. U.S.-Pakistan relations, vital to the war effort, were deteriorating owing to ongoing American drone attacks in Pakistan. And an Afghan national parliamentary election in September demonstrated once again that Afghanistan had a long way to go in achieving fair elections and that President Hamid Karzai continued to tolerate corruption on a large scale.

The result in the U.S., amplified by mounting monthly death tolls, was rising discontent, both within Congress and the general public. A national Bloomberg poll in July found that 58% of Americans considered the war effort a "lost cause," while Gallup tracked a steady rise in the percentage of Americans who believe sending U.S. forces to Afghanistan in 2001 was a mistake, from 30% when Obama took office to 38% in 2010.

None of the year's setbacks came as a particular surprise in a situation that has proved intractable—except

Targets *U.S. troops patrol a village west of Lashkar Gah in Helmand province in southern Afghanistan on Feb. 10, three days before Operation Moshtarak was formally launched*

for the abrupt departure of General McChrystal. The four-star general was brought down by his own hand—or mouth—thanks to a *Rolling Stone* magazine article published in late June that contained quotes in which the general and his staff loudly and eagerly dissed leaders of the Obama Administration. The President quickly fired McChrystal and named counterinsurgency specialist General David Petraeus to replace him.

Despite the early success of the Marjah campaign and the advent of General Petraeus, the overall military situation did not improve during the summer. In September, as a national parliamentary election approached, TIME's Jason Motlagh reported that the Taliban-led insurgency remained entrenched in the southern and eastern provinces and had gained ground in the north, which had previously been relatively stable, while inflicting record casualties on U.S. and international forces, swollen by the 30,000-strong troop surge ordered by President Obama in 2009.

Late summer brought more bad news. Internet exposé site WikiLeaks released a trove of some 91,000 classified documents on the war, which painted a depressing picture of the extent of ISI involvement with the Taliban. That news confirmed the findings of a paper by Matt Waldman of Harvard University's Carr Center for Human Rights Policy called "The Sun in the Sky," published in July. From

Allies *Secretary of State Hillary Clinton attended a conference in Afghanistan and met with President Karzai on July 20*

February to May 2010, Waldman had conducted separate interviews with nine active Taliban field commanders in Afghanistan and 10 former Taliban officials. The commanders, Waldman reported, were unanimous in their belief that the ISI was running the Taliban insurgency, despite the cooperation Pakistan showed earlier in the year in arresting Mullah Baradar.

The September election illuminated the size of the task ahead. Only some 40% of registered voters showed up at the polls, with about 1 million fewer votes cast overall than in 2009's flawed presidential election. Meanwhile, attacks against voters and polling places were carried out in half of the country's 34 provinces, and accounts of fraud and corruption at the polls were everywhere.

In mid-October NATO officials confirmed that President Karzai had begun holding peace talks with the Taliban, a situation that once might have looked like a betrayal of U.S. interests but now was seen by some observers as a shortcut to the end of a war that is costing the U.S. $100 billion a year for limited strategic returns.

In 2006, when the war in Iraq was faltering as an election approached, President George W. Bush sought to delay any serious debate over military strategy until after voters went to the polls. Months later, he announced an entirely new approach, the so-called surge. Three and a half years later, in a different theater, Obama advisers designated December 2010, a month after the midterm elections, as the next point at which the Administration would conduct a full review of strategic progress. In the meantime, the conclusion drawn by TIME's Michael Scherer in July still seemed all too applicable. "The news from Afghanistan has been negative for a while," he wrote, "and there are still no signs of a turning point." ∎

Obama advisers designated December 2010, a month after the midterm elections, as the next point at which the Administration would conduct a full review of strategic progress

Taking over *General David Petraeus receives a flag of command of the war in Afghanistan at a July 4 ceremony in Kabul*

Pakistan: The Primary Concern. Afghanistan's neighbor may hold the keys to peace in the region

Calling card
Pakistani soldiers fire mortar rounds across the border into Afghanistan early in 2010, during training maneuvers

FOR MANY OBSERVERS, PAKISTAN REPRESENTS A SIDE-show to the conflict in Afghanistan. But TIME's national political correspondent Joe Klein argues that it's the other way around. "Afghanistan is really the sideshow," he wrote in July. "Pakistan is the primary U.S. national-security concern in the region. It has a nuclear stockpile and lives under the threat of an Islamist coup by some of the very elements in its military who created and support the Taliban."

Why are elements of the Pakistani military supporting the Taliban? In a word, India—first and last, the strategic obsession of the Pakistan military. The U.S. has come and gone from the region in the past; the perceived Indian threat is eternal. With the defeat of the Taliban by U.S. forces in 2001, Pakistan feared that the new government in Kabul would be sympathetic to India and provide a strategic base for anti-Pakistan intelligence operations. So Pervez Musharraf, then Pakistan's dictator, helped keep the Taliban alive. Under current President Asif Ali Zardari, the nation's ISI security force remains deeply involved with the Taliban insurgency in Afghanistan.

The politics in the region are in flux. In the fall of 2010, relations between Pakistan and the Karzai government warmed after Karzai removed his intelligence chief, Amrullah Saleh, whom the Pakistanis considered an Indian agent. There was talk of a reconciliation deal in which the Haqqani Network, the most radical Taliban group, would stand down militarily. And after a series of spectacular terrorist attacks inside Pakistan, the army launched a major campaign against the indigenous Taliban.

Even as Islamabad and Kabul drew closer, the U.S. and Pakistan found themselves at odds over ongoing U.S. drone strikes on Pakistani soil, which Pakistanis view as a severe violation of their sovereignty. On Sept. 30, Pakistan closed a key border crossing NATO uses to ship supplies to Afghanistan after a U.S. helicopter attack killed two Pakistani soldiers, despite a U.S. apology. The closure left hundreds of trucks, many carrying fuel, stranded alongside the country's highways, and some 150 of them were soon put to the torch by gunmen. The crossing was opened on Oct. 9. Meanwhile, Islamabad was rife with rumors of a possible army coup against Zardari's regime. As usual, little in the region seemed predictable, except that it would remain unpredictable. ∎

On the spot *Pakistan's Zardari speaks at the U.N. in September, with a picture of his slain wife, Benazir Bhutto, at his side*

No winner *Campaign posters bedeck a Baghdad street a week before the March 7 parliamentary election. No majority emerged, and a government was still taking shape as of November*

Turning a Page in Iraq

To little fanfare, the last U.S. combat troops depart, leaving behind a government in limbo and an emboldened opposition

ON THE NIGHT OF AUG. 31, PRESIDENT BARACK Obama addressed Americans from the Oval Office for only the second time in his presidency, a sign of the importance he and his aides placed on his message. And his remarks indeed marked a turning point in the history of two nations, the U.S. and Iraq. "Tonight," the President declared, "I am announcing that the American combat mission in Iraq has ended. Operation Iraqi Freedom is over, and the Iraqi people now have lead responsibility for the security of their country." Two weeks before, Obama noted, the U.S. Army's 4th Stryker Brigade had departed Iraq for Kuwait, the last American combat troops to leave the nation.

The 7-year U.S. combat mission in Iraq ended with a distinct sense of anticlimax, TIME correspondent Bobby Ghosh reported from Baghdad. No triumphant banner was unfurled on the bridge of an aircraft carrier as the troops departed, but the soldiers heading home could be forgiven their sense of exultation. They had accomplished their mission; it was not their fault that it had been redefined over and over again during the seven years and five months of combat operations. Whatever their political masters required of them, they unfailingly delivered. Smash Saddam's army? Check. Crush the Shi'ite Mahdi Army? Check. Wrest Fallujah from the Sunni insurgency—twice? Check and check. Make friends with the same insurgents to defeat al-Qaeda? Check. They weren't ordered to finish that job, however, and their pullout was greeted by the terrorists, as expected, with celebratory carnage: bombs exploded in at least 13 Iraqi cities on Aug. 25.

Also incomplete were the many nonsoldiering tasks assigned to the troops. They built schools and sewage systems, disbursed small-business loans and helped irrigate fields, drank bottomless cups of sweetened tea in order to build relationships with tribal elders and city politicians. But they were not given time to consolidate these gains; left unsupported, they may swiftly be lost.

Nearly 50,000 uniformed U.S. service personnel remained in Iraq to provide training and other services. They are not designated combat troops but are armed and ready to be deployed should combat become necessary. The Aug. 25 bombings suggested al-Qaeda and its supporters hoped to exploit both the dwindling of the U.S. military presence and the fecklessness of Iraq's political élite. Indeed, Iraqis voted in a parliamentary election on March 7, but no party won a clear majority of the votes. As Obama spoke, almost six months later, there was still no new government in place, although on Nov. 11 the nation's three competing factions agreed to a power-sharing arrangment in which Prime Minister Nouri al-Maliki and his Shi'ite Islamic Dawa Party would retain control of the government, while Kurdish leader Jalal Talabani would remain as President and Suuni leader Osama al-Nujaifi would be Speaker of the Parliament.

There's ample reason to believe that the Iraqis will get it right in the end: theirs is a modern nation, rich in resources both human and material. But few doubted that things may get much worse before they get better. There was little celebration among Iraqis as the last U.S. combat brigade rumbled down the highway to Kuwait, only a sense of exhausted resignation. Halfway across the world, those feelings were echoed by the U.S. public, whose attention had shifted from the Middle East to a nagging recession and an election of their own. So ended Operation Iraqi Freedom. If any nurses were kissed by any sailors, no cameras recorded the smooch. ∎

"Our combat mission is ending, but our commitment to Iraq's future is not."

—PRESIDENT BARACK OBAMA

When Johnny comes flying home *Soldiers from the Virginia National Guard's 1st Battalion, 116th Infantry Regiment, prepare for takeoff from Tallil Air Base outside An Nasiriyah*

Talking Peace

U.S.-led peace negotiations are a struggle as Israelis balk and the Palestinians lack leverage

New cycles *Above, Israeli kids play at the Ma'aleh Adumim settlement in the West Bank near Jerusalem. The future of such Israeli outposts was a central issue as Netanyahu, Clinton and Abbas met in Washington to talk peace in September, right*

FOR VETERAN WATCHERS OF THE MIDDLE EAST, IT was déjà vu all over again: a U.S. President was shaking hands with Israeli and Palestinian leaders while a respected U.S. Secretary of State and special envoy looked on, as talks began in Washington in hopes of forging a peace settlement in the troubled region. Meanwhile, a concerned Israeli public scrutinized the talks closely, clinging to frantic hopes for peace.

Or ... maybe not. On Sept. 2, even as President Barack Obama opened a new round of direct talks between Israeli PM Benjamin Netanyahu and Palestinian Authority President Mahmoud Abbas, TIME correspondent Karl Vick reported that the first direct negotiations in two years were met with a collective shrug in Israel. "The truth is, Israelis are no longer preoccupied with the matter," he reported. "They're otherwise engaged."

Asked in a March poll to name the "most urgent problem" facing Israel, just 8% of Israeli Jews cited the conflict with Palestinians, putting it fifth behind education, crime, national security and poverty. For Israel's Jews, the issue that President Obama calls "critical for the world" just didn't seem ... critical. "There is no sense of urgency" about the peace process, Tamar Hermann, a political scientist, told Vick. Hermann has measured the Israeli public's appetite for a negotiated settlement every month since 1994, the year after the Oslo Accords seemed to bring peace so close, Israelis thought they could touch it. They couldn't. It flew farther away in 2000, when Yasser Arafat turned down a striking package of Israeli concessions at Camp David. What came next was the second *intifadeh*, a watershed of terror for an Israeli majority that, amid waves

of suicide bombings, saw no reason to keep hope alive.

The concrete wall Israel erected on its eastern side during the second *intifadeh* sealed out not only suicide bombers but almost all Palestinians. An Israeli Jew can easily spend years without meeting one. In the West Bank, the territory administered by Abbas, technocratic Prime Minister Salam Fayyad is taking a serious stab at governance, starting by professionalizing security forces. The Gaza Strip, sealed off by Israel and ruled by Hamas, has been largely quiescent since a thunderous retaliatory Israeli military operation ended in January 2009.

The "final status issues" at the talks were the borders of a Palestinian state, the question of Jerusalem and the fate of Palestinians who fled their homes six decades ago. But the real test came over the ongoing building of settlements by Israel in the occupied territories. Netanyahu had alienated the hard-line right-wing parties whose support keeps his coalition government in power, when in November 2009 he imposed a 10-month moratorium on

5/31/10

Intervention at Sea.
Israel stops an aid flotilla—at a cost

Angered by the 2006 victory of Hamas in elections in Gaza—and the pounding of rockets from the Palestinian territory that followed—Israel imposed a nautical blockade on the waters off the territory. In May, a flotilla of boats organized in Turkey by foes of the embargo set sail for Gaza. The six vessels carried medical aid and construction supplies. On May 31, as the six ships were in international waters approaching Gaza, Israeli warships intercepted them and commandos dispatched from helicopters and speedboats boarded them. Five of the ships were seized without incident, but Gaza supporters aboard flotilla flagship *MV Mavi Marmara* put up a fight. In the brief skirmish that followed, nine activists were killed and dozens injured, while seven Israelis were wounded.

As the Gaza supporters had hoped, the incident drew international attention to the ongoing blockade, and a chorus of voices around the globe condemned the Israeli action. A U.N. report assailed the Israelis' "unacceptable level of brutality," while Turkish-Israeli relations, once friendly, went into a deep freeze, with Turkey recalling its ambassador. Israeli authorities responded by slightly loosening the land blockade that has helped keep aid supplies out of Gaza.

such construction in the West Bank, where some 300,000 Israeli Jews have settled. That ban helped jump-start the talks, but when it expired in late September, Netenyahu refused to renew it, and the talks lagged. In November, after an 8-hour negotiating session with Clinton, Netanyahu agreed to a one-time only 90-day extension of the ban, in exchange for $3 billion worth of military equipment and assurances that the U.S. would block any Palestinian attempt to obtain international recognition unilaterally at the U.N. The settlement ban opened a short window for progress, but a larger settlement—between Israelis and Palestinians—seemed far out of reach. ∎

Interception *Israeli commandos stop and board one of the aid ships bound for Gaza*

Man of the hour *Campaign workers from Erdogan's AKP party pass out literature urging a yes—or* evet—*vote in Istanbul before the September constitutional-reform election*

Recep Tayyip Erdogan

Turkey's Prime Minister is turning his nation to the East—and some Turks fear that he is turning himself into a strongman

AT THEIR GREAT TRIUMPHS, ROMAN EMPERORS wary of hubris had a slave repeatedly whisper into their ear, "Remember, you are mortal." For Turkish Prime Minister Recep Tayyip Erdogan, 56, a similar memento mori was delivered by basketball fans in Istanbul on the evening of Sept. 12, just hours after he had won a decisive referendum to reform the country's constitution: as he arrived to watch the final of the world-championship game between Turkey and the U.S., Erdogan was greeted by boos. "Nobody can stand in the way of Erdogan now," columnist Mehmet Yilmaz wrote the next day in the mainstream *Hurriyet* newspaper. "What Turkey will see now is a series of steps that will turn him into Putin."

For Erdogan's supporters, comparisons to Russia's autocratic leader are just sour grapes from sore losers. The reforms, designed to curb the outsize political influence of the Turkish military and judiciary, were approved by 58% of voters in the referendum, which had a high turnout. But the booes and the 42% no vote were stern reminders that many Turks are suspicious of the reforms and of Erdogan. They are wary of his authoritarian streak—he has been nicknamed "Sultan Erdogan"—and question his motives. They have criticized him for cherry-picking European Union–inspired reforms only when it allows him to trim back his two biggest secularist opponents, the military and the courts. Those two institutions see themselves as custodians of Turkey's secularism and have repeatedly clashed with Erdogan. As recently as 2008, the country's top court almost banned his Justice and Development Party (AKP), which has strong Islamist underpinnings, for antisecularism, as it had several previous parties with religious affiliations.

It is the Establishment secularist judges who may be the biggest losers in the September vote. The most controversial of the approved reforms paves the way for political appointments by parliament and the President to Turkey's highest court, which controls most senior judicial appointments. Critics worry that the government will use the changes to name religious conservatives to important positions.

To understand what is happening in Turkey now, a little history is vital. After the Ottoman Empire collapsed at the end of World War I, the modern state of Turkey was forged by a charismatic general, Mustafa Kemal Ataturk, who committed the new nation to Western ways and introduced state secularism to purge what he saw as backwardness. Ataturk banned religious garb and schools, changed from the Arabic to the Latin alphabet and introduced women's rights.

For many years, generals, backed by judges, enshrined Ataturk's secular legacy in an ideology known as Kemalism and used it to attack anything deemed to violate state interests. But the old Kemalist structure of Turkey has been fraying for 20 years. Erdogan's party represents an increasingly affluent, pious middle class—the so-called Islamic Calvinists—rooted not in Istanbul, with one foot in Europe, but in once economically backward regions of Anatolia. In 2010 Europe is still Turkey's largest trading partner, but the European Union is mired in recession, while business with the Middle East and Africa is booming.

Erdogan, a devout Muslim, brash former football player and fiery orator, swept to power in 2002, promising change after years of weak coalition governments. Though schooled in hard-core political Islam, he and his friends learned from numerous Islamist predecessors who had been banned from politics for antisecularism. They broke with the Islamist Old Guard, billed themselves as center-right and founded the AKP on a media-friendly, pro-business platform. They spoke no longer of Islamic unity but of links with Washington and recruited former leftists to gain credibility.

In 2005 Turkey won the right to start talks to join the European Union. Armed with a political mandate, Erdogan's AKP passed a series of democratic reforms, got the economy racking up an impressive 6% average growth over five years and began to chip away at the military's many powers. But the E.U.—led by skeptics on Turkish membership such as French President Nicolas Sarkozy and German Chancellor Angela Merkel—has increasingly turned its back on Ankara.

In response, Erdogan and Foreign Minister Ahmet Davutoglu have pursued a strategy of greater involvement in the Middle East, though their hopes of establishing Turkey as a mediator in regional disputes have thus far come to naught. The country's relationship with Israel collapsed following the deadly Israeli raid on Turkish aid ships heading to Gaza in May. Shortly after that incident, Turkey voted against a U.S.-sponsored resolution at the U.N. Security Council imposing sanctions on Iran. The next day, Ankara announced an economic pact with Jordan, Syria and Lebanon to create a free-trade zone.

After his party's September victory, Erdogan declared that he would seek a new, more democratic constitution if he is re-elected in 2011, when he is widely expected to win a third term. Whether or not Erdogan becomes a new Putin—or a new Caesar—he and his nation are determined to become major players in a region that is rapidly changing. Turkey, says Erdogan, "can no longer be taken for granted." ■

"Nobody can stand in the way of Erdogan ... What Turkey will see now is a series of steps that will turn him into Putin."

—MEHMET YILMAZ, NEWSPAPER COLUMNIST

Designs on the Future.
With a flashy exposition in Shanghai, China reaches out to the world

MOST OF THE PLANET'S CITIES WERE BATTLING SLUGGISH economies in 2010, but not Shanghai. On a June night, TIME's Justin Bergman reported, groups of giggling, camera-toting visitors, young and old, dashed from pavilion to pavilion at the Shanghai Expo 2010 with an excitement usually reserved for roller coasters, not exhibitions of Turkmenistan's industrial prowess. Outside the most popular venues—those of Japan, South Korea, Spain and the U.S.—thousands lined up patiently, waiting for up to two or three hours for a chance to get in. Children flashing *V* signs with their fingers posed for photographs with Haibao, the jaunty blue expo mascot that bore an uncanny—some might say deliberate—resemblance to Gumby. Bereft of visitors, however, were expo outcasts North Korea and Iran, whose pavilions were dull tributes to the nations' economic and infrastructural developments. The venues stood beside each other in a desolate corner of the grounds. A sign of China's shifting loyalties, perhaps?

China
The host nation's pavilion was the largest and costliest ($220 million) at the exposition. Designed by He Jingtang, it sought to evoke the feeling of an ancient Chinese crown.

CHINA PHOTOS—GETTY IMAGES

CHINA PHOTOS—GETTY IMAGES

United Kingdom
The $36 million pavilion, left, designed by Thomas Heatherwick, was a "Seed Cathedral," a striking orb pierced by 60,000 slender transparent rods, each holding a different seed. But, one visitor told TIME, "inside there is nothing to see!"

CHINA PHOTOS—GETTY IMAGES

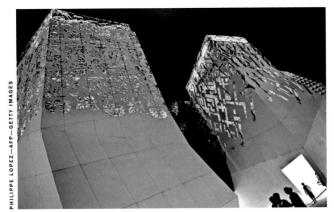

South Korea

Designed by Mass Studies, the pavilion, left, featured characters of the Korean alphabet on its exterior; this is its indoor/outdoor entrance.

Russia

The pavilion's 12 towers rose to perforated, illuminated tops. Designed by P.A.P. ER, it was Russia's first newly built expo pavilion in 30 years.

The Netherlands
The jazzy Dutch pavilion, nick-named "Happy Street," was designed by John Kormeling. It featured typical Dutch houses —and a miniature soccer field.

Saudi Arabia
The $164 million pavilion, designed by a team of Chinese and Saudi architects, evoked the prow of an oil tanker with a palm-shaded oasis on its deck.

Malaysia

The pavilion, left, was based on designs used by the vast nation's Minangkabau ethnic group on West Sumatra. The *rumah gadang* ("big house") style features steep gables crossing at a lower, central junction.

Switzerland

The exterior of the pavilion, designed by Buchner Bründler Architects, was laced with solar-powered LED lights that sparkled as energy was produced and consumed. Inside, a cable-car ride took visitors past projected views of the Alps.

Denmark

Designed by the Bjarke Ingels Group, the Danish pavilion led visitors down a winding gyre of a walkway that resembled a ski slope; at its bottom was the famed sculpture of Hans Christian Andersen's *Little Mermaid*, appearing for the first time outside Denmark. The building also promoted sustainability and energy efficiency.

The odd couple *New Prime Minister David Cameron, left, a Conservative, prepares to take charge of Britain's government, sharing power with Deputy PM Nick Clegg, a Liberal Democrat*

David Cameron and Nick Clegg

When Britain's May election ended in a hung Parliament, two former foes became allies and formed a coalition government

AS THE COUPLE STEPPED OUT THROUGH THE French doors and past trailing wisteria to the sun-flecked lawn of 10 Downing Street in London, where their guests awaited on gilded chairs, someone said in a stage whisper, "It's just like a wedding." And so it was: love—or at any rate, amity—hung in the scented air as Britain's new Prime Minister, David Cameron of the Conservative Party, and his surprising political paramour, Deputy Prime Minister Nick Clegg of the Liberal Democrats, held their first joint press conference since taking office on May 11. There were even anecdotes embarrassing enough to (dis)grace any best man's speech. Did Cameron regret his past answer to the question "What is your favorite

joke?" a journalist asked. Cameron's riposte, amusing enough at the time and even more so with the benefit of hindsight, had been "Nick Clegg."

That revelation—clearly news to Clegg—may have put the first dent in the duo's shiny new relationship, forged when British voters went to the polls on May 6 and split their votes so effectively between Cameron's Conservatives, Clegg's Liberal Democrats and the Labour Party led by sitting PM Gordon Brown that the balloting ended in Britain's first hung Parliament since 1974. Five days of feverish horse-trading followed, culminating in an agreement between Cameron and Clegg, previously bitter opponents, to form a coalition government.

Another irreverent question from a reporter hinted at the underlying seriousness of establishing clear lines of authority: "If the phone rings at 3 in the morning, will you both answer it?" What already seemed clear, however, was a chemistry between the two and a shared excitement about their new project in joint government, "an administration," said Cameron, "united behind three key principles: freedom, fairness and responsibility." He went on to reveal that he and Clegg had discussed forming a looser working partnership, a so-called confidence and supply agreement, in which the Liberal Democrats would have supported the Conservatives on key issues but not joined the government. Cameron said that he and Clegg had discussed such an arrangement but rejected it as "so uninspiring."

More than four years after his surprise victory in a Tory leadership contest made him the leader of his party and despite the remorseless scrutiny that comes with his position, Cameron took power as still something of an enigma to his countrymen: affable, clubbable but strangely unfathomable. At 43, he is the youngest occupant of 10 Downing Street since the early 19th century. He's posh—he went to Eton, the toniest of all English boarding schools—and his wife Samantha, creative director of luxury-goods brand Smythson, is posher still, a descendant of King Charles II. Most Britons seemed to forgive these accidents of birth and allow Cameron and his wife to present themselves as just another young, metropolitan couple.

The Camerons entered Downing Street with two children; in 2009 they had suffered the death of their severely disabled son Ivan, who was then 6. That tragedy, and the experience of Ivan's short life, helped reshape Cameron's ideology. "It has a big influence on you if you have a disabled child and you spend a lot of time in hospitals with social workers and respite-care workers," he told TIME in 2008. "It brings you into touch with a lot of people you meet in politics, but you meet them in a different way." Amid all his campaign vows to begin tightening his nation's belt, Cameron quietly promised to shield Britain's taxpayer-funded National Health Service.

On Aug. 24, Samantha Cameron gave birth to the couple's fourth child, daughter Florence Rose Endellion. Only two weeks later, Cameron's father Ian passed away, capping a tumultuous year in the young leader's political and personal life.

Nick Clegg's ascent to power was the most surprising aspect of the election. Britain's electoral system, like the one used in U.S. congressional elections, disadvantages third parties such as the Liberal Democrats, whose support is widely distributed. "Almost 1 in 4 people voted for us last time, and we got, what, 10% of the seats in this place," the Cambridge-educated Clegg, 43, told TIME in an interview in his House of Commons office in February.

At the time, the sheer improbability of the Liberal Democrats' acquiring real power had dampened media interest in the party, and Clegg was fighting for attention. He got plenty of that following an electoral innovation based on U.S. politics, a nationally televised debate among the three party leaders on

A journalist asked, Did new Prime Minister David Cameron regret his past answer to the question "What is your favorite joke?" Cameron's riposte had been "Nick Clegg."

April 15. Clegg emerged a clear winner after effectively hijacking what one might call the hopey-changey message hitherto monopolized by Cameron, and British voters entered a period variously dubbed by tabloid newspapers as "Cleggmania" and "Cleggstasy."

The mania faded before the election, perhaps after British voters were reminded that Clegg is a passionate pro-European, a former employee of the European Commission and former member of the European Parliament. He is also the scion of a Dutch mother and a half-Russian father; his wife Miriam González Durántez is Spanish; and their kids have distinctly non-Anglo names—Antonio, Alberto and Miguel.

The result was the hung Parliament and the new relationship between Cameron and Clegg. The two face enormous challenges in pursuing their declared goal of cutting Britain's public spending by 25% in four years. But on that first shared visit to 10 Downing Street, the future seemed filled with hope. "This is what new politics looks like," said Clegg, stretching out his arms, as if to embrace the whole garden and all the people in it, even the journalists. The honeymoon promised to be brief, but most Britons seemed to be wishing the best for the happy couple. ∎

In Brief

Burma

THE LADY WALKS FREE *On Nov. 13 the tough military regime that rules Burma (Myanmar) released its most persistent foe—and the world's most famed political prisoner—Aung San Suu Kyi, 65, from house arrest after a seven-year term ran out. The daughter of Aung San, the man who liberated Burma from British rule after World War II, had served 15 of the past 21 years in confinement. Suu Kyi, winner of the Nobel Peace Prize in 1991, pledged that she would continue to apply pressure for democratic reforms in Burma. A week earlier, Burma held its first national elections in two decades; the expected victory for the regime was widely dismissed as bogus.*

Iran

A Surprise Cyber-Attack

A new era in the annals of warfare may have dawned in July 2010, when accounts first emerged that a powerful computer worm had struck nuclear plants in Iran. The malware, christened Stuxnet, has been described as the most powerful tool of cyberwar yet developed. It was discovered by a Belarus-based agency performing security work on Iranian computers. *PC World* and other sources reported that specialists who studied the bug believed the worm had been tailored to attack computers running software designed by German engineering company Siemens. Iran's top nuclear plant in Bushehr, left, employs Siemens equipment and is believed to have been the primary target in the attack, though the worm has been found in other nations.

Experts said the Stuxnet program was so advanced and complex that its creation could only have been funded by a nation-state. Reports from within Iran were sketchy, and as of the fall of 2010, the extent of the damage done to Iran's nuclear operations remained unknown—as were the authors of the Stuxnet virus itself.

Leaders
Rising Tide

Women rose to positions of power across the globe in 2010. On Oct. 31, Dilma Rousseff, below, the chosen successor to popular President Luiz Inácio Lula da Silva, won 56% of the vote in a runoff election to become the next President of Brazil. Lula's former chief of staff will take office on Jan. 1, 2011.

A former Vice President under Nobel laureate Oscar Arias Sánchez, Laura Chinchilla of the National Liberation Party, won 47% of the vote in a February election to become Costa Rica's first female President.

On Sept. 7, Julia Gillard, 49, became the first woman elected Prime Minister of Australia, after striking a deal with independent representatives to give her Labour Party a 76-to-74 majority in Parliament. Voters in Iceland, Croatia and Lithuania had chosen female heads of state in 2009.

North Korea

Stirring Up Trouble

On Nov. 23, North Korea fired artillery shells across a disputed maritime border at Yeonpyeyong Island, killing two South Korean Marines and two civilians, injuring 19 people and setting more than 50 homes ablaze. The South scrambled fighter jets and returned artillery fire. The skirmish followed the March 26 sinking of the South Korean warship *Cheonan*, killing 46 seamen, which the South blamed on the North.

On Sept. 30, North Korea released the first photographs of the newly anointed successor to leader Kim Jong Il, now 69 and ailing. The choice: Kim's third and youngest son, Kim Jong Un, above, who is believed to be 26 or 27.

Britain

A Royal Wedding for 2011

Putting an end to years of speculation, Britain's Prince William of Wales, 28, second in line to the throne after his father Charles, announced on Nov. 16 that he would wed his longtime sweetheart, Kate Middleton, 28. The vows will take place on April 29.

China

A Dissenting Voice, Prized

Despite repeated warnings from the Chinese government, the Nobel Committee named jailed Chinese dissident writer Liu Xiaobo winner of its 2010 Peace Prize on Oct. 8, citing "his long and nonviolent struggle for fundamental human rights in China." Liu, 54, had been in prison since Christmas 2009, when he was sentenced to 11

years for criticizing China's communist government in a widely circulated petition dubbed Charter 08, which calls for free speech and other human rights.

Soon after the award was announced, President Barack Obama, the recipient of the 2009 Peace Prize, called on China to release Liu, saying that political reform in the country "has not kept pace" with "dramatic progress in economic reform."

Yemen

An Airborne Bomb Plot Fails

On Oct. 29, two bombs hidden inside the toner cartridges of Hewlett-Packard desktop printers made their way from Sana'a, Yemen, via FedEx and UPS to cargo hubs in Dubai and Britain, traveling some of the way in the holds of passenger aircraft. They were intercepted just hours short of takeoff for Chicago.

The attack could have killed hundreds onboard those planes. It might have succeeded if not for a tip from Saudi intelligence that led to the discovery of the bombs. The plot exposed flaws in the global cargo-security system, and in its wake, the Department of Homeland Security announced new restrictions on air freight: cargo from Yemen and Somalia will be blocked, and large printer cartridges will be banned from passenger flights.

The bombmaker was believed to be Ibrahim al-Asiri, a Saudi working with al-Qaeda in the Arabian Peninsula. That group, led by American-born jihadist Anwar al-Awlaki, right, is believed to have also staged the attempted bombing of an airliner on Dec. 25, 2009.

Foiled *Explosive materials were found within desktop printers shipped as airplane cargo*

Life

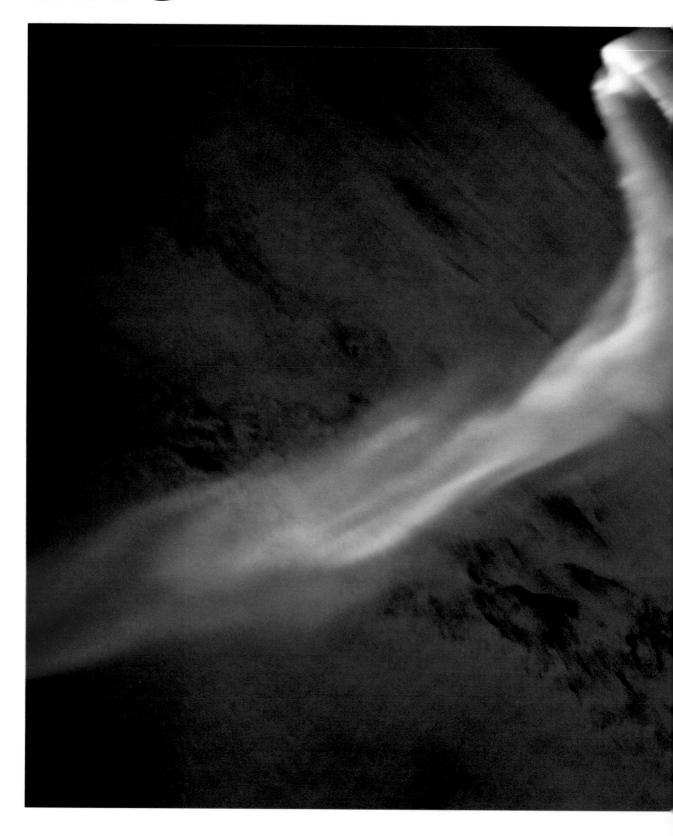

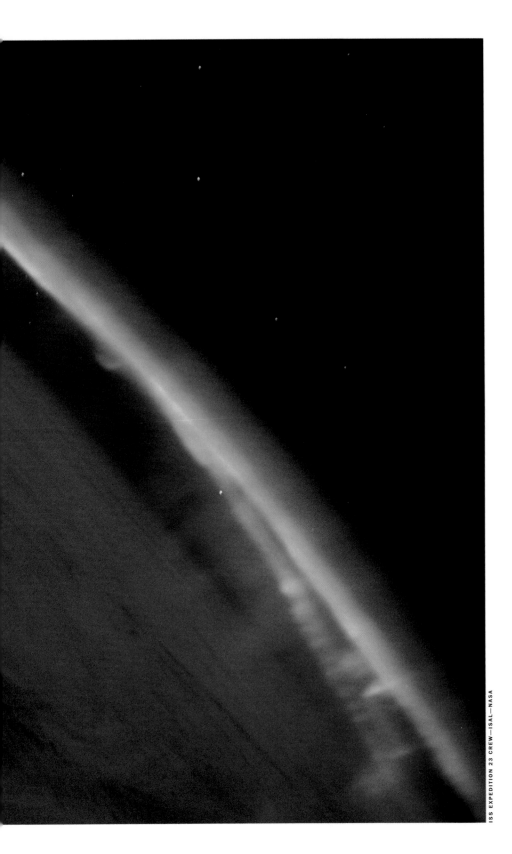

Solar Power

Planet Earth's two polar auroras— the aurora borealis (northern lights) and aurora australis (southern lights)— offer magnificent, luminous displays to those in polar latitudes. But the view of the auroras from outer space is even more spectacular, showing the vast size they can reach. At left is a picture of the aurora australis taken on May 29 by astronauts aboard the International Space Station. The vivid hues are formed when charged particles released by the sun in the form of coronal mass ejections collide with our planet's magnetosphere, exciting oxygen atoms and making them glow.

TOP ROW, FROM LEFT: SHAUL SCHWARZ—EDIT BY GETTY IMAGES; JUAN

Nature's Horrors

Deadly disasters afflict
millions across the globe

HAITI 1/12/10

FOR LONG-SUFFERING HAITI, 2010 WAS A
year of exceptional agony. Late in the afternoon of Jan. 12, a 7.0 earthquake lev-
eled the capital city of Port-au-Prince and
its surroundings in the greatest national
disaster in the nation's history. The temblor not only
struck a country mired in poverty; it attacked its
nerve center. It erupted just 15 miles (about 24 km)
from the capital, rendering its seaport unusable, its
airport barely functional and its roads snarled by
debris and the homeless. The bureaucratic decapita-
tion meant that aid and personnel initially had to be

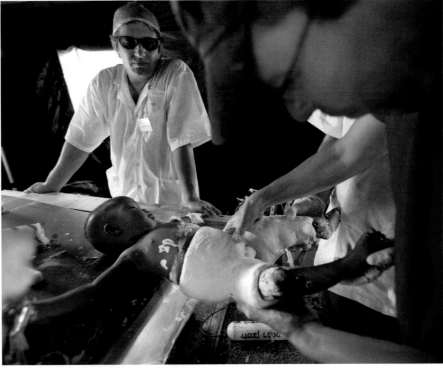

Scenes from a Nightmare

In the top row, far left: Natalie Tijor, who lost both her parents in the quake, mourns in the streets. At center, downtown Port-au-Prince is a shambles two days after the temblor. At right, doctors apply a cast to an infant injured in the disaster.

After the Disaster

At far left, police break up a looting spree in the capital five days after the quake struck. At center, bodies are left at a cemetery for burial. At right, Floria Loveng, 7, hugs a friend in a tent city of displaced citizens.

shipped in, either through the neighboring Dominican Republic or secondary airports in Haiti.

For all the uncertainty and chaos in the early days following the quake, it was clear the world wanted to help. From the high-level work of former President Bill Clinton, the U.N. special envoy to Haiti, who was later joined in the aid effort by former President George W. Bush, to the millions of dollars donated through text-messaging, there was no shortage of generosity in response to the devastation. Americans alone gave more than $190 million in the first week after the quake. In Haiti, emergency medical teams operating out of shipping containers worked to save limbs and lives, and desperate requests went out to U.S. medical schools for more volunteers. The final toll of the disaster may never be known, as tens of thousands of corpses were delivered to mass graves without notice. By September, international agencies estimated the earthquake had left some 250,000 people dead, 300,000 injured and more than 1 million homeless.

The pace of reconstruction was agonizingly slow, and by the fall hundreds of thousands of Haitians were still living in makeshift tent communities. They were prime targets for a cholera epidemic that began in November: by Nov. 22, officials estimated that some 1,200 Haitians had already died from the bacterial disease, and there were more than 19,500 cases around the country.

Eyjafjallajokull Erupts

THE RUMBLES BEGAN IN 2009, BUT IT WASN'T UNTIL APRIL 14 of 2010 that Iceland's big volcano, Eyjafjallajokull, began percolating with significant power, spewing gigantic columns of ash into the sky. As volcanoes go, the eruption of the 5,466-ft. (1,666 m) Eyjafjallajokull, or Eyja, for short, won't make the history books. Scientists measured it at 2-3 on the Volcanic Explosivity Index, which ranks volcanic events on a 1-to-8 scale. Eyja's blast barely compared with major eruptions like Mount St. Helens in 1980, which killed 57 people and devastated hundreds of square miles of forest, or the catastrophe of Krakatoa in Indonesia in 1883, which killed more than 40,000 people and was felt around the world. By contrast, Eyja's eruption caused no deaths, and just 800 people living near the volcano had to be evacuated.

But the medium-sized eruption on tiny Iceland—an island formed by ancient eruptions that sits atop one of the planet's largest tectonic rifts—had an enormous impact on the world. As its 7-mile (11.3 km) -high plume of volcanic gases and silicate ash spread across much of Europe, it brought air travel across the Continent to a near standstill for 6 days in some places: volcanic emissions can clog jet engines and lead to crashes. Delays and cancellations hit airports from Toronto to Tokyo, and the problems were estimated to have cost the global air-travel industry $200 million a day. Not bad for a minor-league eruption.

The havoc caused by Eyja is a reminder that in our interconnected world, it's less the sheer power of a natural disaster than where and when it happens—and how prepared we are to respond—that matter. If the volcano had erupted in the years before air travel became common, it wouldn't have been noticed outside Iceland.

The same goes for other kinds of natural disasters. The Haiti earthquake in January 2010 killed some 250,000 people, yet it registered only a 7.0 on the Richter scale—strong but not that strong. In fact, it barely compared with the 8.8 temblor that hit Chile a little more than a month later, killing fewer than 500 people. What's the difference? Population density—the Haiti quake struck the country's capital of Port-au-Prince, whereas the one in Chile missed big cities like Santiago—and preparation. Chile is a relatively well-off South American nation with a long history of earthquakes, so its buildings are designed to resist seismic waves, and the government

and people know how to respond. Impoverished Haiti, by contrast, was helpless, and its people paid the price.

As global populations have grown and people have crowded into risk zones such as earthquake areas and floodplains, the toll of natural disasters has grown as well. According to the Center for Research on the Epidemiology of Disasters, the number of catastrophic events has more than doubled since the 1980s, and the Red Cross estimates that the economic damage from disasters rose fivefold from 1985 to 2005. Despite appearances, volcanoes and quakes are not getting worse; rather there are more of us living in areas where we might be affected by a disaster, and we have more to lose than ever before.

Going Up
Horses outside Fimmvorduhals, Iceland, pay no heed to the towering column of smoke, ash and other matter erupting from Eyjafjallajokull on April 16.

Bedding Down
At right, Huw Thomas, a Briton, eats breakfast on a cot at John F. Kennedy International Airport in New York City, his flight plans scuttled by a faraway eruption.

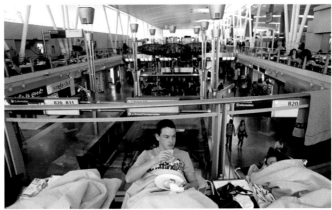

PAKISTAN 8/1-31/10

Floods Swamp Pakistan

THE MONSOON RAINS THAT COME EACH YEAR ARE THE lifeblood of India, Pakistan and southeast Asia, bringing the water that sustains people and crops in one of the planet's most populous regions. But in 2010 the monsoons in Pakistan were much heavier than usual, and in August the nation's rivers became raging torrents, breeding misery rather than renewal. The floods hit first in the northwest, wiping out much of the region's infrastructure, and then the bloated rivers gushed toward the south and the east, killing more than 1,700 people and affecting as many as 20 million more, in one of the planet's greatest natural disasters of recent years.

The floods, centered on the swollen Indus River, set off a chain reaction of catastrophes. Raging floodwaters swept away roads and bridges, stranding millions of people beyond the reach of aid workers. They also damaged hundreds of health facilities and displaced an estimated one-third of the country's 100,000 female health workers, who provide primary medical care to millions of rural Pakistani women.

Relief efforts were agonizingly slow, hindered by the devastation to the nation's infrastructure. As Pakistan's army, local charities and international agencies scrambled to organize a unified response to the tragedy, Pakistanis heaped abuse on their government, whose initial response was chaotic and inept. President Asif Ali Zardari defended his administration's efforts to alleviate the misery, while predicting that full recovery would take a minimum of three years.

The U.S. quickly pledged a massive $200 million relief package and mobilized swift on-the-ground assistance. In the first weeks after the floods began, some 20 U.S. military helicopters working out of Ghazi in northern Pakistan and three C-130 aircraft making daily runs from Bagram in Afghanistan delivered more than 2.4 million lbs. (1.1 million kg) of relief supplies and airlifted more than 8,800 people from flood-affected areas. As correspondent Rania Abouzeid reported in TIME, these efforts were welcomed by politicians and the media, yet many Pakistanis remained suspicious of U.S. motives, seeing the relief efforts as more political than humanitarian. For its part, the Pakistani Taliban urged citizens to reject any foreign aid, saying it would only be stolen by the nation's political leaders. Jihad, it would seem, does not pause for calamity. ■

Aid from the Sky
At top, in this picture shot from a Pakistan army helicopter, the blue objects at right are water bottles being dropped to flood victims stranded on a small island of high ground amid swollen waters.

Color and Chaos
At far left, displaced villagers line up for food in a relief camp near Muzaffargarh in the Punjab.

City of Refugees
Near left, homeless citizens are sheltered in a relief camp in Sukkur in the Sindh province in Pakistan's hard-hit north.

A Census of The Oceans

There's lots of good fish in the sea, and we're still discovering them

ONLY THE SEA KNOWS THE DEPTH OF THE SEA." SO goes a line from Hindu scriptures, one that well describes the mystery of the ocean depths—and our ongoing ignorance about life beneath the waves. For thousands of years, our knowledge of the seas was limited to surface currents and the fish that we could catch, close to the coast. We knew little of what lived below the depth a man could dive, and often imagined the deep ocean to be an aquatic desert, undifferentiated and mostly devoid of life. It was only in the 19th century that scientists began to look deep: in the 1870s the H.M.S. *Challenger* performed a remarkable around-the-world scientific voyage, dredging amazing creatures from the deep. But even today, our knowledge of the deep seas and what lives there is still a sketch. Almost 20% of the oceans' volume has never had a single scientific sample taken from it.

Now that's beginning to change, thanks to one of the most silently remarkable scientific research programs ever launched. In October at the Royal Institution of Great Britain in London, scientists presented the findings of the initial Census of Marine Life, a 10-year-long, $650 million initiative that attempted—for the first time—to systematically catalog what lives in the world's oceans. The international project involved more than 2,700 researchers from 80 nations, who spent a total of 9,000 days at sea during at least 540 expeditions. They found and described some 1,200 new species (right, with genus and species names and general type) and collected 5,000 more that have yet to be classified. The most ambitious act of marine science in history took advantage of advances in genomics that allow for rapid DNA screening of new organisms. Yet it still hasn't come close to plumbing the depths of the sea's mysteries. Scientists used to believe there were some 250,000 species in the sea; following the census, they expanded their estimate to at least 1 million and perhaps 2 million. As veteran oceanographer Sylvia Earle explained to TIME's Bryan Walsh, "We don't even know what we don't know." ∎

Lysianassoid amphipod (crustacean)
Off Elephant Island, Antarctic Ocean

Dinochelus ausubeli (crustacean)
South Pacific Ocean

Metapseudes sp. (medusa)
Off Western Australia, Indian Ocean

Alviniconcha sp. (vent snail)
Tokyo Hydrothermal Vent, Pacific Ocean

Bathykorus bouilloni (medusa)
Arctic Ocean

Leptocheliidae sensu lato (shrimp)
Great Barrier Reef, South Pacific Ocean

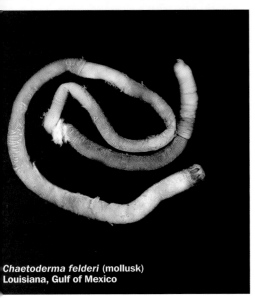

Chaetoderma felderi (mollusk)
Louisiana, Gulf of Mexico

"Squidworm" (still unclassified annelid)
Celebes Sea, Southeast Asia

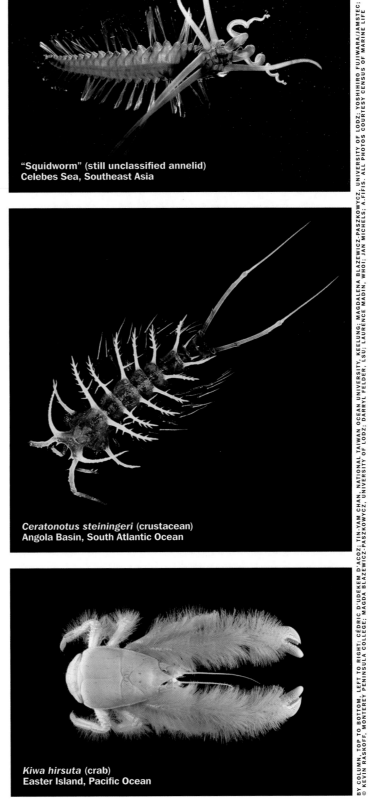

Ceratonotus steiningeri (crustacean)
Angola Basin, South Atlantic Ocean

Kiwa hirsuta (crab)
Easter Island, Pacific Ocean

BY COLUMN, TOP TO BOTTOM, LEFT TO RIGHT: CÉDRIC D'UDEKEM D'ACOZ; TIN-YAM CHAN, NATIONAL TAIWAN OCEAN UNIVERSITY, KEELUNG; MAGDALENA BLAZEWICZ-PASZKOWYCZ, UNIVERSITY OF LODZ; YOSHIHIRO FUJIWARA/JAMSTEC; © KEVIN RASKOFF, MONTEREY PENINSULA COLLEGE; MAGDA BLAZEWICZ-PASZKOWYCZ, UNIVERSITY OF LODZ; DARRYL FELDER, LSU; LAURENCE MADIN, WHOI; JAN MICHELS; A.FIFIS. ALL PHOTOS COURTESY CENSUS OF MARINE LIFE

Lab Report
Nutrition, Science and Medicine

Football: Fun for the Fans, Bad for the Brain

FOOTBALL HAS BEEN A ROUGH SPORT since the leather-helmet days, but today's version raises the violence to an art form. No other contact sport gives rise to as many serious brain injuries as football does. High school football players alone suffer 43,000 to 67,000 concussions per year, though the true number is likely much higher, as more than 50% of concussed athletes are suspected of failing to report their symptoms.

Repeated blows to the head, routine in football, can have lifelong repercussions. A study commissioned by the NFL found that ex–pro players over age 50 were five times as likely as the U.S. national population to receive a memory-related-disease diagnosis. Players 30 to 49 were 19 times as likely to be debilitated.

For years the NFL downplayed any link between football head trauma and cognitive decline. Finally, in 2010 the league acknowledged the problem and took the first steps toward addressing it: now an NFL player who sustains a concussion cannot return to the game that day. But medical experts say that far more radical reforms must be undertaken—and soon.

The World Health Organization advises women who miscarry to wait at least six months before getting pregnant. But new research from Scotland found that women who conceived within six months of miscarrying had the best chance of a successful pregnancy. The age of the women may have been the driving factor in the study: the longer older women wait to try again, even by a few months, the higher their risk of having another miscarriage.

One more reason not to let a stranger into your bed

BEWARE, HUMANS! Nearly eradicated for the past half-century in the industrialized world, bedbugs—a.k.a. *Cimex lectularius*—are on the rise in the 21st century. How to fight them? DDT kills 'em dead, but the bugs developed a resistance to DDT decades ago, before the poison was banned. One pesticide, propoxur, kills adult bedbugs within 24 hours and keeps killing newborns as they hatch. But the U.S. Environmental Protection Agency banned propoxur for in-home use in the 1990s. For home infestations, the EPA recommends reducing clutter, sealing cracks and crevices, vacuuming often, drying infested clothes at high heat and using a special mattress cover—so you can sleep tight without letting the bedbugs bite.

Americans scramble to deal with salmonella-tainted eggs

THE GREAT EGG SCARE BEGAN on Aug. 13 with a recall of 228 million eggs tainted by salmonella, but it expanded to cover half a billion eggs produced by two Iowa companies, the largest such recall in U.S. history. The outbreak began just after the Food and Drug Administration's new regulations for egg-safety production, created in 2009, went into effect. They include testing, sanitation and refrigeration requirements for egg operations and allow the FDA to inspect farms for compliance.

DATA SET

50% Extent of greater odds that people with strong social connections will live longer than those with weak ones

20 Number of bottled-tea drinks needed to equal the health-boosting polyphenol content of one cup of green or black tea

EXERCISE

Attention, joggers: it's time to put more sole in your run

A GROWING NUMBER of trainers and scientists believe that ditching cushioned soles may be the best way to protect joggers against chronic injuries. In a December 2009 issue of a journal put out by the American Academy of Physical Medicine and Rehabilitation, researchers concluded that running in shoes exerts more stress on the knee, hip and ankle than does running barefoot or walking in high heels. One alternative for those who don't dare to go bare: the goofy-looking, but effective, thin rubber foot gloves that coddle your toes and protect tender soles from debris.

NUTRITION

Organic eggs: yes, they're more expensive, but are they really better for you?

EVEN BEFORE A SALMONELLA OUTBREAK focused attention on the safety of factory-produced eggs, organic-besotted Americans were turning backyard chicken coops into a status symbol. With exquisite timing, the U.S. Department of Agriculture released a study in June of the difference between factory-produced and free-range eggs—and found that they were indistinguishable.

Yet the President's Cancer Panel Report released in May exhorted consumers to choose food grown without pesticides or chemical fertilizers, antibiotics, and growth hormones. Looks like Uncle Sam's agencies are playing a game of chicken.

9 Number of U.S. states with an obesity rate of 30% or higher, up from three states in 2007. More than 1 in 4 Americans are obese

Parents whose kids can't seem to tear themselves away from the Internet often wonder: Can pathological Web surfing trigger depression? According to a survey of Chinese high school students, the answer is yes. Scientists found that healthy teens who used the Internet obsessively—reporting that they felt moody or nervous when not online—were 2.5 times as likely to become depressed nine months later as were less frequent Web surfers.

FINDINGS

Studies in Better Health

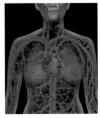

WOMEN AND THE HEART

Heart disease is the leading killer of women in the U.S., each year claiming more women than men. Yet because too many women remain unaware of the danger, physicians at the Mayo Clinic and women living with heart disease have teamed up to spread awareness of the problem. Each year, 50 to 70 women gather for a four-day series of lectures and emotionally charged discussions with some of the clinic's leading heart specialists. Then these WomenHeart champions, as they are called, return to their communities to advocate for heart health—including spreading awareness that heart-attack symptoms in women are very different from those experienced by men.

TO TAX OR NOT TO TAX?

Americans' growing problem with obesity has led to increased calls to place a tax on sugary thirst-quenchers. A study released in July by the U.S. Department of Agriculture's Economic Research Service concluded that hiking the price of sugar-sweetened soda, juice and sports drinks by 20% could cut the percentage of adult Americans who are overweight from 66.9% to

62.4%. The findings came on the heels of a controversial study published earlier in the year in the journal *Health Affairs* that concluded that small-scale increases in the cost of soda would likely have little impact on childhood obesity.

TO STAY HEALTHY, SHAKE OFF THE SALT

A study by researchers at the University of California, San Francisco, Stanford University and Columbia University shows that even a modest decrease in daily salt intake can lead to major health benefits. The authors found an annual drop of as many as 120,000 cases of heart disease, 66,000 instances of stroke and 99,000 heart attacks caused by high blood pressure after a 3-gram-per-day reduction in sodium. The advantages were more profound for African Americans, who are more likely to develop high blood pressure and may be more sensitive to the hypertensive effects of salt than other ethnic groups, and for the elderly, since blood vessels stiffen with age, raising blood pressure.

Hard truths *Mulally told* TIME *that when he took the reins at Ford, he asked his new colleagues, "You guys lost $14 billion last year. Is there anything not going well here?"*

Alan Mulally

No, he's not a "car guy," but under this can-do former Boeing executive, Ford Motor is spreading its wings

LISTEN TO FORD MOTOR CO.'S EXCITABLE CEO, Alan Mulally, for five minutes and you're almost ready to march to the assembly line, grab a torque wrench and start knocking bolts into Mustangs. "We are fighting for the soul of American manufacturing," Mulally told TIME's Bill Saporito. "We are leading the way on What does it take for America to compete in the global economy? That's what this is about. And it starts with making the best products in the world.

After the industrial Armageddon that left GM and Chrysler in bankruptcy, Mulally's Ford is flying the flag of resurgence. The company earned $2.6 billion on sales of $31.3 billion in the second quarter of 2010. Its market share jumped 1.4 points, to 17.5%, at the expense of GM and Chrysler. In the Kelley Blue Book rankings, Ford claimed the top spot from troubled Toyota as the best-regarded auto brand in the U.S.

Pulling off the biggest business turnaround of the Great Recession has been strong second act for Mulally, 65, who arrived at Ford in late 2006 after 37 years at Boeing, amid sniping that he wasn't a "car guy"—as if the car guys in Detroit were doing a bang-up job. In 2010 Ford unveiled three new cars that may put more distance between it and the rest of the crowd. A new Fiesta, designed in Germany, is sporty, smart, thrifty and cool. The new Explorer is an SUV reborn as a more fuel-efficient vehicle built on a Taurus platform, as opposed to its former gas-gulping truck frame. The Focus will be the first global car built from the ground up based on Mulally's signature strategy, known as One Ford, which means selling the same model, built the same way, in all markets.

One Ford means that the very definition of what a Ford is—steering, handling, the sound of a door slamming shut—may change as the company's global DNA evolves. "One spin in a Fiesta will tell you as much: it's as much Milan as it is Milwaukee," reported Saporito. As Ford changes gears from world-class survivor to world-class automaker, Mulally is showing that he is a car guy—just his own kind of one. ∎

Julian Assange

The founder of WikiLeaks argues that he opposes all censorship, but his primary goal seems to be embarrassing governments

JULIAN ASSANGE IS ABOUT TO SIT DOWN WITH TIME's Eben Harrell to explain how his website, WikiLeaks.org, came to publish more than 90,000 secret reports from the wars in Afghanistan and Iraq when he starts to get restless. His chair is made of soft leather, and Assange doesn't like it. "There's no hard surface to slam my fist on and say, 'F_____ bastards! I will crash them all!'" he says, smiling. It's hard to tell whether Assange is joking. A tall, wan, white-haired former computer hacker, Assange is so soft-spoken, it is sometimes difficult to hear him. But just a day earlier, on Aug. 9, 2010, his website released a log of documents that exposed in unprecedented detail the difficulties NATO troops face in Afghanistan. The publication of the classified documents made headlines around the world, as did the release of leaked data on the Iraq war in late October.

On a roll, Assange and WikiLeaks caused more headaches for the U.S. government by releasing a trove of some 250,000 diplomatic documents on Nov. 28, including 15,000 marked "secret." Although no major state secrets were revealed, the cables provided hard evidence of what has long been suspected but not officially stated: Arab leaders have urged military action against the Iranian nuclear program; senior Afghan officials are deeply corrupt; the U.S. has tried to offload Guantanamo detainees on resistant countries, and so on.

Assange, 39, is a child of the Internet age. The Australian broke into the master terminal of Nortel, the Canadian telecom company at age 20. Apprehended, he pleaded guilty and paid only a small fine after a judge complimented his "intelligent inquisitiveness." He studied physics at the University of Melbourne as an adult student, and now moves between four bases—which he does not specify, citing security concerns.

Assange founded WikiLeaks in 2006 to help whistleblowers post confidential material anonymously. The group consists of six full-time volunteers and about 1,000 part-time encryption experts; its main server is in Sweden, though the operation is global. "I have tried to invent a system that solves the problem of censorship of the press and the censorship of the whistle-blower across the whole world," he told TIME. But for governments, he was creating problems, not solving them. As leaders across the globe denounced WikiLeaks, Assange was playing an increasingly dangerous game—and had become the world's most wanted man. ◼

Hidden truths *Assange lives on the run, believing he is frequently tailed*

Toyota's Tough Ride

Executives hang their heads and consumers wring their hands
as the world's No. 1 automaker recalls some 9 million vehicles

Fixing the problem *A mechanic prepares a recalled Toyota Prius for brake-system diagnosis and repair in Norwood, Mass.*

Accepting the blame *Nakabayashi Hisao, president of Toyota's Korean unit, bows in apology for recalls in Korea*

AS AN EXERCISE IN POLITICAL THEATER, THE HOUSE Energy and Commerce Committee hearing on Feb. 23 into the troubles plaguing Toyota, the No. 1 automaker in the world, had everything you could hope for: testy exchanges, Clintonian hairsplitting, obnoxious grandstanding, tearful testimony and even multiple references to Marisa Tomei's automotive wizardry in *My Cousin Vinny.* The spectacle demonstrated that while U.S. Representatives may have trouble passing laws these days, they remain masters at displaying indignation. But it failed to untangle the knottiest question looming over the proceedings: whether Toyota had definitively pinpointed the problems that were causing its cars to accelerate out of control. Toyota vehicles have been involved in some 2,600 instances of sudden, unintended acceleration and 34 deaths since 2000.

Toyota insists that many of the acceleration incidents were the result of driver error. Yet even so, those concerns, and some additional design and manufacturing flaws, resulted in a major embarrassment for a company that had built its reputation on reliability. By hauling the top brass of the largest automaker in the U.S. to Capitol

Hill for a public flogging, House members got to vent their outrage at Toyota's sclerotic response to the crisis.

Toyota's woes began when it issued a recall for some 4.9 million cars in September 2009. But recall followed recall, until, by the end of January 2010, the once revered company had called back more than 8 million vehicles to fix issues ranging from faulty brakes to troublesome floor mats to sticky gas pedals.

On Jan. 27, Toyota finally slammed on the brakes, announcing it had elected to indefinitely halt sales of eight models, including the Camry, America's best-selling car,

> **"Toyota has, for the past few years, been expanding its business rapidly. Quite frankly, I fear the pace at which we have grown may have been too quick."**
>
> —AKIO TOYODA, TOYOTA CEO

Eyeing the future *A futuristic Toyota Prius hybrid is ready for its close-up at the 80th Geneva Car Show in March*

and the Corolla, the practical compact model on which the Japanese automaker built its reputation for quality and durability. Executives suspended production at five U.S. plants, idling more than 20,000 workers and leaving 1,200 Toyota dealers sitting with roughly 250,000 unsold vehicles in their lots. Analysts suggested that it might take years for the company to regain the consumer confidence it had taken decades to earn.

On the second day of the House hearings, Akio Toyoda, the company's president and CEO—and grandson of its founder—offered up a heavy dose of contrition. "Toyota has, for the past few years, been expanding its business rapidly," he said. "Quite frankly, I fear the pace at which we have grown may have been too quick." Yoshimi Inaba, Toyota's top executive in the U.S., tried to put a positive spin on the crisis, saying Toyota hoped to use the recalls to impress customers with its service.

Surprising analysts, on Aug. 4, Toyota posted a $2.2 billion profit for the second quarter of 2010. But the troubles continued: in October, Toyota recalled 1.5 million cars to fix leaking brake fluid—perhaps an all too apt metaphor for the automaker's runaway quality problems. ∎

Current Events. Is the time finally right for electric cars to charge?

The future of the automobile is electric—or so we've heard for decades. But 2010 may be remembered as the year the plug-in revolution finally arrived, as automakers began rolling out a bevy of electric models. GM launched its long-awaited and much hyped electric Volt, below, for about $40,000, with federal tax rebates that knocked the price down to $32,500. Around the same time, Nissan began selling its all-electric Leaf, a $32,780 compact that the Japanese carmaker says will average 100 miles (161 km) on a charge, and Daimler began leasing an all-electric version of its Smart Car. BMW, Chrysler, Ford and Mitsubishi, among others, plan to release electric models by the end of 2011. Even Toyota, long a proponent of hybrids, announced in May 2010 a venture with Tesla, whose $101,000 electric roadster is popular with Silicon Valley moguls, to develop electric-car technology in California.

Huge roadblocks remain. How many drivers will be willing, or able, to charge their cars 7 or 8 hr. a day for only 100 or so miles of driving? More than a few will surely suffer from the dreaded "range anxiety"—worrying that they will run out of juice in the middle of nowhere. Price is an issue too. Electrics cost considerably more than comparable gasoline-powered cars and are too expensive for the average buyer. The good news: electric-car technology is advancing quickly, and the price is dropping as it does. If the revolution continues, your Honda Accord may someday need a cord.

iPad, iSold, iConquered

Steve Jobs and Apple launch a tablet computer that quickly becomes a hit—and Apple tops Microsoft in net worth

Tablet *Jobs shows off the iPad's sleek, mouseless design at the product's unveiling. The tablet weighs 1.5 lbs. (.68 kg) and is 9.5 in. tall, 7.5 in. wide and 0.5 in. deep (24 cm x 19 cm x 1.3 cm)*

ONCE UPON A TIME, THERE WAS A VERY RICH, very clever man. He got up on a big stage and held up a new kind of computer. It was flat, and it didn't have a keyboard. This very rich, very clever man then tried to convince a bunch of reporters that in five years this flat, keyboardless computer would be the most popular kind of computer in the country. Some of them even believed him.

The year was 2000. The man's name was Bill Gates.

That year at Comdex, which at the time was the biggest technology trade show on the calendar, Microsoft unveiled something it called a Tablet PC. Just for good measure, the company unveiled it again at Comdex in 2001. But it never caught on: the Tablet PC was much like a piece of paper, except it was heavier and more expensive, and it broke when you dropped it. Nor was it alone. Scores of notebook computers followed it in failing to capture the imagination of the public.

Until 2010, that is, when another very rich, very clever man stood before a cheering throng of gearheads (and a few skeptical journalists) on Jan. 27 to unveil yet another tablet computer. But this time around, the computer guru was the charismatic Steve Jobs, and the tablet was dubbed the iPad. Within 80 days, consumers who have come to expect Jobs' company, Apple Computer, to create transformative technology made the iPad a big hit, buying 3 million of the slim, streamlined devices.

The release of the iPad was the highlight of another remarkable year for Jobs and Apple: the company also updated two previous breakthrough devices, the iPhone

and the iPod. And on May 26, Apple reached a major milestone: for the first time, its net worth as measured by its Wall Street market value topped that of its longtime rival, Gates' Microsoft. It was a moment of validation for Jobs, 55, who had been forced off the Apple board in 1985, and for his company, widely written off as a second-tier has-been around the turn of the millennium.

The iPad uses the multitouch screen technology, pioneered for the iPhone, that allows the user to enlarge and reduce the screen display and employ programs with the tap of a finger. Its battery runs for 10 hours before it needs charging. More important, the iPad is merely the tangible component of a much larger device, an entire Internet ecosystem that extends out to the horizon in every direction. Other companies can't match Apple's skill in constructing media pipelines for its products. As of 2010, designers had created some 250,000 apps (applications) for the iPhone system, and the iPad promised to be just as app-friendly an environment.

When he unveiled the iPad, Jobs also touted Apple's new iBooks online retail site, which the company hopes will transform the publishing industry, just as its iTunes store changed the music business. Indeed, the iPad is designed to be a serious rival to Amazon's popular Kindle e-book reader, and newspaper and magazine publishers are hoping the new device may finally create a paradigm for paid delivery of digital journalism.

Then there's the touchy-feely factor. As TIME's Lev Grossman wrote, "Conventional PCs live in studies; laptops make brief, furtive forays into the living room. The iPad will become the first whole-house computer, shared among an entire family, passed from hand to hand, roaming freely from living room to kitchen to bedroom ... at ease everywhere, tethered to nothing. It's not a revolution, but it's a real change, the kind of change you notice."

As for Apple's breakthrough iPhone, its 2010 update provided amusement for the geek world when a company employee accidentally left a prototype of the new-model iPhone 4 in a Silicon Valley beer garden. Computer site Gizmodo got ahold of it, showing pictures and analyzing the phone weeks before Apple was scheduled to unveil it. The notoriously secretive Jobs made light of the incident when he debuted the new smart phone on June 7: "Stop me if you've seen this before," he told the audience. But Jobs wasn't smiling when the phone's nifty new antenna, which is built into its outer case, was found to lose power if a key transmission point was covered by a user's hand. Apple quickly offered new buyers free carrying cases that corrected the problem.

By the time Jobs unveiled Apple's new line of updated iPods in the fall, the verdict was in: the maestro had done it again in 2010. Apple was bordering on irrelevance and financial ruin when Jobs rejoined it in late 1997. How he ruthlessly refocused the company—cutting projects he deemed worthless, doubling down on others and reaching for a future that he not only saw but made happen—will be a subject that business pundits will be dissecting for decades ... very likely on their tablet computers. ■

The iPad is merely the tangible component of a much larger device, an entire Internet ecosystem that extends out to the horizon in every direction

The Year in Technology.
Online chats and DVD rentals, 2010 edition

CHATROULETTE

The year's hottest new website was Chatroulette, a platform for live, face-to-face conversations with total strangers, with few rules and no guidelines. The site took anonymous online chatting (not a new thing), added webcams and let users have at it. Chatters don't need a user name, a profile or a friend request to take part—there's an immediate connection to a random stream of total strangers from all around the world. Bored by what you see? Click "Next," and someone else is waiting. Too often, however, that person was waiting in the buff, for the uncensored site quickly became a haven for voyeurs and, uh, voyeurees.

Fittingly, the racy online playground was the brainchild of a teenager, 17-year-old Muscovite Andrey Ternovskiy, who said he coded the site himself, with hosting for the project funded by family and friends. The site now supports itself through a small line of advertisements at the bottom of the screen. Launched in November 2009, the site was attracting 35,000 users at a time within three months, with male users heavily outnumbering females.

REDBOX

Redbox, the DVD rental company, is one of the Great Recession's success stories. Its $1-a-night DVDs can be returned to any of Redbox's 22,400 kiosks, often located in supermarkets, McDonald's, pharmacies and strip-mall parking lots. Fail to return it, and the most you will be charged is $25—about the cost of a new DVD. In 2009 Redbox added one new location per hour and made twice as much in revenue—$774 million—as it did in 2008. Redbox and online renter Netflix spelled red ink for store-based Blockbuster, which filed for bankruptcy in late September.

In Brief

Environment

ASIAN INVASION *Above, Asian carp leap from the water, spooked by a motorboat's engine, while fishermen haul them in on the Bath Chute by the Illinois River. But local humans are also spooked: non-indigenous Asian carp have invaded the Mississippi River as well, where they've crowded out native species. Now they're poised to infiltrate the Great Lakes, where these ravenous plankton-eaters and prolific breeders could ravage the native ecosystem and disrupt a commercial and sport fishery worth billions of dollars. In July several Great Lakes states filed a federal lawsuit to force the Army Corps of Engineers to step up its anticarp measures, and the White House named a "carp czar."*

Society

Bullying Ends a Promising Life

Tyler Clementi, right, an 18-year-old freshman at Rutgers University in New Jersey, took his life on Sept. 22 after his roommate and a friend allegedly conspired to broadcast a dorm-room tryst between Clementi and another man on the Internet, using a hidden camera. Clementi, a gifted violinist, jumped from the George Washington Bridge in New York City. The suicide came as Rutgers was launching "Project Civility," intended to suppress bigotry and cyber-bullying on campus.

While prosecutors weighed pressing charges against Clementi's alleged tormentors, a legion of gay celebrities took to YouTube to assail the attack and counsel young gay people to reach out for aid in the face of such behavior. "Things will get easier, people's minds will change, and you should be alive to see it," said TV host Ellen DeGeneres.

Education

Jefferson Jettisoned

On March 12 the Texas state board of education voted 10 to 5 in favor of curriculum standards that would promote politically conservative takes on controversial issues in the state's history textbooks, including an increased emphasis on and sympathetic treatment of such Republican Party touchstones as the National Rifle Association and the Moral Majority. The new books will also tout the superiority of capitalism and

the role of Christianity in the nation's founding. Thomas Jefferson's profile will be diminished; some board members were less than fond of his ideas about the separation of church and state. In September the board voted to reduce coverage of Islam in the schoolbooks.

Religion

The Vatican: Still Under Fire

Pope Benedict XVI's Vatican was beset by new charges in 2010 that church leaders had covered up sex crimes against youngsters committed by predatory priests. The spotlight fell most strongly in Belgium, where a lengthy independent report suggested that 13 suicides may have followed such abuse. Visiting Britain in September, the Pope offered his strongest apology yet for the church's lack of vigilance. Members of the Survivors Network of those Abused by Priests gather at Vatican City, below.

Energy

Diurnal Odyssey

The *Solar Impulse* took wing, powered by the sun, on July 7, in Switzerland. Then, using solar energy it saved from the daylight hours, it flew right through the night, landing after 26 hours. The ultralight, one-person craft has 12,000 photovoltaic cells on the upper wing surface. Next step, say its designers: a round-the-world flight.

Architecture

Getting High In Dubai

There's a fine line between confidence and hubris, and perhaps Dubai and its real estate developers crossed it when they planned the Burj Khalifa. The hotel complex, which opened its doors in January 2010, is by far the world's tallest building at 2,717 ft. (828 m). One hitch: since the 160-floor skyscraper was planned, the tiny emirate's go-go boom had stalled, and its real estate bubble had popped. Sheik Khalifa bin Zayed al-Nahyan, the oil-rich ruler of neighboring Abu Dhabi, stepped in with $10 billion to stave off an embarrassing default, and the skyscraper's grateful owners changed the tower's name to Burj Khalifa.

On the list of the 10 tallest buildings in the world, only Chicago's venerable Willis (formerly Sears) Tower represents the older, developed economies; the other nine are now in Asia and Dubai.

Business

The Skies: A Tad Too Friendly?

In September stockholders of United Airlines and Continental Airlines approved a $3 billion merger that had been pending for more than two years, creating what will be the world's largest airline. The merger will cut capacity in the sky, and for flyers that's expected to mean fuller planes and higher prices, analysts said. After Delta completed a merger with Northwest early in 2010, fares on their combined routes rose some 10%. Bon voyage!

Leisure

A New Way to Get Your Kicks

Kickbikes combine a bicycle's body and handle-bars with a pedal-free platform to stand on and big fat tires. They're a fast, fun way to cross-train, run errands, commute and even help rehabilitate injuries. Stroke patients like them (they require using just one side of the body), as do dog lovers eager to keep up with frisky pooches. Americans buy about 15,000 a year, vs. 15 million bicycles, but this fad has, uh, leg.

Sport

Narrow Escape

Mike Conway, racing for the team of Dreyer & Reinbold, flies through the air after crashing with Andretti Autosport driver Ryan Hunter-Reay during the 94th running of the Indianapolis 500 auto race in Indianapolis on May 30.

The crash took place during the final lap of the race, which was won by Dario Franchitti of the team owned by Chip Ganassi. Both Hunter-Reay and Conway gambled that they had enough fuel to finish the final lap, but when Hunter-Reay ran out of gas and slowed, Conway hit his car and the vehicle flipped. Hunter-Reay suffered a broken leg and a fractured vertebra in his neck, while two spectators were treated for minor injuries.

The Games That Soared

After a shaky start, Vancouver's Winter Olympic Games achieved lift-off

OVERSIZED, OVERENGINEERED AND OVERHYPED, THE OLYMPIC Games are the Hummers of the sports calendar. And as the world's attention turned to the Vancouver Winter Games early in 2010, the question had to be asked: With nations around the globe battling economic woes, could the Olympics once again summon their golden aura? Early on, the auspices were not good. An unseasonably warm winter threatened to turn the Alpine events into mud derbies. The day of the opening ceremonies, luger Nodar Kumaritashvili from the Republic of Georgia was killed when he lost control of his vehicle on a course that experts had warned was too fast to be safe, casting a pall on the celebration. And a global TV audience was stunned when the opening ceremonies were marred by a technical glitch, and the torch-lighting ritual that is the emotional high point of the Games was a letdown. For can-do Canada, a nation renowned for its courteous efficiency, the foul-up was glaring.

Yet when the attention turned from made-for-TV spectacles to athletics, the Games asserted their grip. The snows came, and new-age sports like snowboarding and freestyle skiing, once scorned as exotic interlopers, now seemed part of the backbone of the Games. Fans in the U.S. found a bevy of heroes to root for, from "old-timers" like snowboarder Shaun White, 23, and speed skater Apolo Anton Ohno, 27, to new faces like the men's gold medalist in figure skating, Evan Lysacek. Women's figure skating offered yet another enchanting champion, South Korea's elegant Kim Yu-Na. The host Canadian teams won gold medals in both men's and women's hockey, proof that the gods of Olympus were pleased with the contests. And when it came time to quench the winter flame for another four years, the Canadian organizers playfully mocked their glitch from the opener, proving that these good sports know how to put on a good show. Far from a Hummer, Vancouver's Games were a humdinger. ∎

Gravity's Reigning Bro

U.S. snowboarder White, a born showman, had already won the gold medal in the half-pipe event, but he saved his best effort for last. In his final run, he unveiled a new move, the dazzling Double-McTwist 1260—and nailed it

BRIAN ADLER 2010/EPA—LANDOV

Stars, Stripes and Smiles
Julia Mancuso, left, and Lindsey Vonn led a strong effort by U.S. downhill skiers. Above, the friendly rivals, both 25, celebrate winning silver and gold in the Alpine downhill event. In her third Winter Games, Vonn also placed third in the Super-G event.

A Tragedy in Training
Georgia's Nodar Kumaritashvili lost control of his luge during a training run on the day of the opening ceremonies, slammed into a concrete support pillar and died. The 21-year-old was traveling at almost 90 m.p.h. Officials ordered immediate modifications to the luge track to prevent further accidents.

Gold on Home Ice

All Canada rejoiced when Sidney Crosby, 22, scored a goal in overtime to beat the U.S. and win hockey gold for the host nation—and that included his teammates. Canada's athletes, buoyed by the financial support of a program dubbed Own the Podium, won 14 gold medals, more than any other national team.

Apolo? Oh, Yes

Short-track speed skating is nasty, brutish—and fast. But U.S. star Apolo Anton Ohno, appearing in his third Winter Games, brings a zenlike calm to the proceedings. Below, he's on his way to a bronze medal in the 1,000-m event. He won two more medals at the Games; with eight medals overall, he is now the most-decorated Winter Olympian in U.S. history.

A Steady Lysacek Skates to Gold
"I don't know when I have ever been so ready for a competition," Evan Lysacek observed before he took the ice in the men's figure-skating final—and he proved it by performing a clean, solid program to beat heavy favorite Evgeni Plushenko of Russia and become the first U.S. men's gold medalist since Brian Boitano in 1988. Lysacek, 24, fared less well when he later appeared, sans skates, on ABC's popular *Dancing with the Stars* show, where he won silver—uh, make that "second place."

Dawn of a New Dynasty?
She may have been only 19 when she competed in Vancouver, but South Korea's Kim Yu-Na, displayed a maturity beyond her years as she outdueled her longtime rival, Japan's Mao Asada, to win the gold medal in figure skating. In what was dubbed the Asian Invasion, skaters from the Far East won five of the 12 gold medals in figure-skating events.

Bode's Hat Trick

He is widely recognized as the greatest U.S. men's Alpine skier ever, but when the Vancouver Games began, Bode Miller's reputation was still suffering from his grumpy behavior at the 2006 Olympics in Italy. Miller, 32, put things right in Canada, winning a gold (super combined), a silver (Super-G) and a bronze (downhill) to add to his two silvers from Salt Lake City in 2002.

The Danes' Diverting Diamonds

For many fans of the Winter Olympics, it's the offbeat events that put the fun in the Games, from the rifle-toting biathlon to Canada's unique amalgam of shuffleboard and skating, curling. At Vancouver, it was the Danish men's curling team, with their snazzy checked drawers, that commanded all eyes. No matter: as expected, Canada whipped the Danes to win the gold. But when Canada's women lost to Sweden, a nation mourned.

When the World Has

SPORTS FANS AROUND THE GLOBE MAY LOVE the Olympics—but they're passionate about the World Cup. And no wonder: the Olympics are Apollo, lighting a torch to summon ancient ideals; the World Cup is Dionysus, face painted, vuvuzela blatting, a hooligan on holiday. So the honors for greatest international sporting event of 2010 clearly belong to soccer, the world's favorite game. The 19th World Cup profited from the risky decision by FIFA, the international body that rules the game, to award the tournament to South Africa. Despite fears that the nation's high crime rate and economic struggles might tarnish the proceedings, South Africans rose to the occasion, offering modern stadiums, safe streets and a colorful backdrop for a noisy, exhilarating tournament.

For U.S. fans, the tournament marked a turning point when that perennial, nagging question—"When is soccer going to be big in America?"—was finally put to rest. Television ratings soared, proving that U.S. fans have made the transition from soccer pioneers to soccer-

a Ball

To the blare of vuvuzelas, South Africa hosts a World Cup to remember

literate and are heading down the road to soccermania.

Running for a month, each World Cup takes on its own dramatic arc. In 2010, the early story line was the weakness of European teams and the ascendance of the South Americans. But on July 11, two European teams who had never won the Cup, Spain and the Netherlands, squared off in the final. One hundred and 16 minutes later, there was joy in Madrid, despair in Amsterdam: Spain won, 1-0. And the world's most devoted sports fans began counting the days until Brazil 2014. ■

The Reign of Spain

At top left, Wesley Sneijder of the Netherlands checks Andrés Iniesta of Spain in the final game. Iniesta scored a goal with four minutes remaining in the 30-minute overtime period to win the trophy.

It Might Get Loud

Ghana's team carried the hopes of African fans deepest into the tournament, eliminating the U.S. team with a 2-1 victory in overtime in the round of 16.

Landon Donovan
Widely considered the best U.S. player, Donovan scored critical goals when they were most needed. At left, the speedy forward celebrates after scoring the winning goal against Algeria to put the U.S. into the round of 16.

Robert Green
Alas, poor Robert. At right, England's goalie got his hands on a kick from Clint Dempsey of the U.S. in the two teams' first game of the Cup—only to let the ball slip away into the net. The goal earned a tie for the U.S., and promised a life of enduring infamy for a gifted athlete.

Lionel Messi
It used to be the Brazilians who played "the beautiful game," but Argentina's renowned wingman, often called the best player in the world, seems to have stolen their grace. Yet even Messi couldn't lead his strong team to the finals.

Kaká
Brazil's talented midfielder led his countrymen to the quarterfinals against the Netherlands, but the Dutch proved too strong for the world's favorite team. Above, Mark van Bommel of the Netherlands, in orange, challenges Kaká.

Diego Maradona
Argentina's legendary player is now the game's most histrionic coach. Jubilant or downcast, he struck dramatic poses and turned his nation's games into a South American–style *telenovela*.

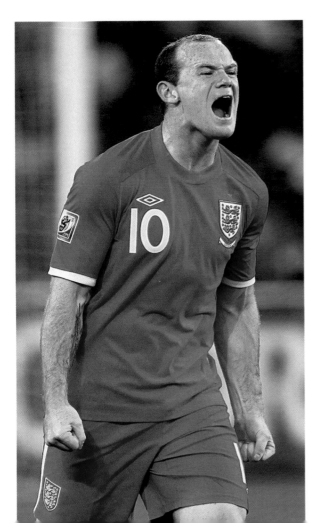

Thomas Müller

The brilliant midfielder, only 20, led Germany to the semifinal round, but Spain prevailed. Above, Müller takes aim during Germany's 3-2 victory over a tough Uruguay team to win third place.

Wayne Rooney

Britain's bad-boy bulldog, one of the world's best strikers, seemed a bit muzzled during the Cup, as did his team. England failed to advance past the second round, and British fans booed their players when they were eliminated by Germany, 4-1.

101

Better red *Nadal's game never looks better than when he plays on the crimson clay courts of the French Open, where he won his fifth championship in 2010*

Rafael Nadal

For years he challenged Roger Federer's reign as monarch of the world's courts—and in 2010 he ascended to the throne

THE RIVALRY BETWEEN RAFAEL NADAL AND ROGER Federer will be recalled as one of the greatest duels in the history of sport. And 2010 marked a turning point in their long conflict, as the exciting Spaniard, 24, took three of the year's four major tournaments, while the suave, unflappable Swiss, 29, began seeming, well, flappable. In June, Nadal won the French Open and took over as the game's No. 1 player in the Association of Tennis Professionals' weekly rankings, which Federer had led for 237 consecutive weeks—a week shy of tying Pete Sampras' record.

The Spaniard's rise to No. 1 ended a period in which Federer's free-flowing and artistic play came as close as humanly possible to achieving perfection within the boxed constraints of a tennis court. Since his first French Open victory in 2005, Nadal's muscular game had helped him consistently beat the Swiss star on Nadal's favorite surface, clay. But in 2008, Nadal came out on top in four meetings, including an epic five-set Wimbledon final that dethroned the grass-court champion in one of the greatest matches ever played. In 2009, Nadal outplayed Federer in the finals of the Australian Open to win his first hard-court Grand Slam title, but the Spaniard's year soon went awry. Federer beat him in the finals of the Madrid Open; then Nadal lost in the quarterfinals on the clay courts of the French Open and bowed out of Wimbledon with a knee injury. Still recuperating, "Rafa" was eliminated in the U.S. Open in the semifinals.

Nadal came roaring back in 2010, although he pulled out of the Australian Open—that knee again—in the quarterfinals. But soon he was hitting on all cylinders, beating Robin Soderling to win the French Open, taking his second Wimbledon championship by whipping Tomas Berdych in straight sets, then winning his first U.S. Open title by beating Novak Djokovic. For tennis fans, it was a bittersweet moment: the sport had a popular new king, but fans longed to see the gifted Federer return to form and give Nadal a run for his money a few more times. ∎

Zenyatta

Move over, Julia and Sandra: America's new sweetheart is definitely faster, arguably prettier—and three decades younger

WHY DO WE LOVE ZENYATTA? LET US COUNT THE ways. We love her because this great Thoroughbred won her first 19 races without a defeat. We love her because she's a female who is widely considered one of the greatest fillies ever to run. We love her because she's larger than life: a full size bigger than most racehorses, Zenyatta stands 17 hands (5.6 ft., or 172 cm) high, making her larger than Man O' War, larger than Secretariat. We love her because of the way she wins: a deep closer, she comes from dead last or next-to-last, eating up ground to pass competitors in the last turn and home stretch to pull out a victory in the final thrilling seconds. And we love her because she's a ham who guzzles Guinness after her training runs and prances in the paddock before each race. Introduced to cheering fans at the Apple Blossom Invitational at the Oak Lawn track in Arkansas in April 2010, she extended her neck to take two deep bows, amazing even her jockey, Hall-of-Famer Mike Smith. She then went last-to-first to win the race going away.

Owners Jerry and Ann Moss (the "M" in A&M Records) named their mare after the 1980 *Zenyatta Mondatta* album by the Police. With trainer John Shirreffs, they held Zenyatta back from the famed Triple Crown events in which American horses make their names, giving her time to mature. She first raced in November of her 3-year-old season at Hollywood Park outside Los Angeles, where she won handily. A string of come-from-behind victories followed, until Zenyatta had won 13 consecutive races, beating such estimable nags as 2009 Belmont Stakes winner Summer Bird and 2009 Kentucky Derby winner Mine That Bird.

Despite her success, some doubters remained. On Nov. 7, 2009, Zenyatta silenced them at the Breeders' Cup Classic at Santa Anita: trapped in midpack of a very strong field as she entered the final turn, she threaded her way to the outside and blazed down the stretch to win, as announcer Trevor Denman cried, "This is un-be-lievable!" Zenyatta was due to retire after that race, but the Mosses relented: at age 6, the mare returned in 2010 and galloped to victory, last-to-first, in her initial five events. The 2010 Breeders' Cup Classic on Nov. 6, 2010, at Churchill Downs in Kentucky was billed as her final run, and once again Zenyatta hung back, trailing by 20 lengths early in the race. And once again she wove through traffic to catch up to the leader, Blame, close to the wire—but Blame nosed her out. Zenyatta's quest for perfection failed, but she will remain the most beloved mare in racing history. ∎

"The Queen" *That's what adoring fans call the great filly Zenyatta, here passing the field to win the Vanity Handicap on June 13, 2010*

Hail to the Victors. The Giants are living large, Kobe is king, and golf goes global

The Giants Win Their First Series in California

The New York Giants divorced their hometown in 1958 and moved to San Francisco, hot on the heels of their longtime foes, the Brooklyn/Los Angeles Dodgers. But unlike the Dodgers, ever since pulling up stakes, the Giants have struggled—until the 2010 World Series, when they trounced a tough Texas Rangers squad to win the fall classic, four games to one. The Giants' pitching star was Tim Lincecum, 26, the long-haired hurler known as "The Freak" (this is San Francisco, remember). Lincecum, hoisted on his teammates' shoulders, above, throws right-handed but bats left-handed. In only his fourth year in the major leagues, he has already won two National League Cy Young Awards, and he pitched the Giants to victory in both the first and fifth games of the 2010 Series.

Kentucky's Sloppy Derby

It rained Friday night and all day Saturday, but just before post time the sun came out at Churchill Downs for the 136th running of the Kentucky Derby. And for the third time in the past four years, the weepy, rail-happy jockey Calvin Borel, 43, brought home a winner, Super Saver, second from right. Lookin at Lucky won the Preakness Stakes, and Drosselmeyer triumphed in the Bemont Stakes.

Racketeers. Serena's still on top, Kim comes back—and Roger shows he's human

Serena Williams

Now 29, the hard-hitting Amazon cruised to easy wins at the Australian Open and Wimbledon, left. But she stumbled at the French Open, and a foot injury left her unable to play at the U.S. Open late in the season.

Roger Federer

The snazzy Swiss, 29, who is widely considered the greatest men's player of all time, got his year off to a good start by winning the Australian Open for the fourth time. But he couldn't seem to summon his past dominance as Rafael Nadal took the year's other three Grand Slam events.

Kim Clijsters

After retiring in May 2007 and giving birth to mini-me daughter Jada, above, early in 2008, the Belgian superstar, 27, returned to the court in 2009. Although unseeded, Clijsters stunned fans by winning the '09 U.S. Open. In 2010 Clijsters successfully defended her crown, defeating Russia's Vera Zvonareva to win her third U.S. Open title.

Room at the Top. With Tiger Woods fighting a slump, rising European stars take three of the game's four top titles

Phil Mickelson

When fan favorite Mickelson won his third Masters on April 11, above, few would have guessed that he would be the only well-known player to win one of the year's four Grand Slam events. "Lefty," 40 in 2010, missed a 1-ft. putt in the second round, but he scored two eagles in the third round and held steady to beat Lee Westwood by three strokes. Westwood got payback, leading Europe's stars to a big win over the U.S. in the Ryder Cup in October.

Graeme McDowell

What a start: when Northern Ireland's rising star won the U.S. Open at Pebble Beach in California at age 30, it was his first victory on the PGA tour. He is the first European to win the Open since 1970.

Louis Oosthuizen

Only a week after the world's eyes turned to Johannesburg for the final game of soccer's World Cup, Oosthuizen, 27, became the fourth South African to win Britain's Open Championship, cruising to victory by seven strokes.

Kobe's Lakers: Still Champs

Once upon a time Kobe Bryant was brash and cocky, locked in a schoolyard rivalry with teammate Shaquille O'Neal. But those days are long past. Bryant, 32, has matured into a leader, and in 2010 he led the Los Angeles Lakers to the NBA finals for the third year in a row. The Lakers faced Boston's Celtics in a classic match-up that went to a full seven games. For the first time in their five seventh-game duels with the Celtics, the Lakers won, 83-79, and Bryant was named MVP of the series. At left, Boston's Paul Pierce and L.A.'s Derek Fisher fight for the ball.

Rogues' Gallery. Once hailed, these stars are now assailed

Tiger Woods

Golf's greatest player fell from grace after a car accident at his Florida home on Thanksgiving 2009 led to his outing as a serial philanderer. Wife Erin Nordegren divorced him, and he couldn't regain his old form in 2010. Above, fans diss Woods, 34, at the Quail Hollow Championship in North Carolina.

Roger Clemens

Widely considered baseball's best pitcher of the past 15 years, Clemens, 48, was indicted by a federal grand jury on Aug. 20. He faces perjury charges relating to his February 2008 congressional testimony, in which he denied using steroids under oath.

Lance Armstrong

The cycling champ, 39, was again accused by a rival, former teammate and admitted doper Floyd Landis, of having using illegal drugs in the past, but the FDA's dogged abuse-hunter Jeff Novitzky has yet to charge Armstrong with using drugs.

FROM TOP: CHUCK BURTON—AP IMAGES; MARK WILSON—GETTY IMAGES; JOEL SAGET—AFP—GETTY IMAGES; JARED WICKERHAM—GETTY IMAGES

Martin Kaymer

Still coming into his own at 25, Kaymer became only the second German to win the PGA Championship, after Bernhard Langer. Rain and fog played havoc with the schedule at Whistling Straits in Wisconsin, before Kaymer beat up-and-coming American Bubba Watson in a stirring three-hole playoff.

Ben Roethlisberger

The Pittsburgh Steelers quarterback, 28, was suspended for the first four games of the NFL season after he was accused of sexually assaulting a college student in Georgia in March. No charges were filed, but the Steeler apologized for his behavior.

In Brief

Hockey

THE ICEMEN COMETH *What if you went to a baseball park in the dead of winter, and a hockey game broke out? That's the premise of the NHL's Winter Classic, which takes pro hockey back to its roots by putting a game on ice around New Year's Day in such stadiums as Boston's Fenway Park, above. The annual outdoor spectacle has helped the NHL recover from a long slump and labor woes, and the league is now on the upswing. In 2010 the Chicago Blackhawks beat the Philadelphia Flyers to win the Stanley Cup, 4 games to 2.*

Basketball

LeBron James Catches Heat

He was Cleveland's No. 1 homeboy (O.K., he hails from Akron, but close enough). Since joining the Cleveland Cavaliers in 2003, the gifted LeBron James, 25, who is a scoring threat from anywhere on the court, has led the team to contending status but never to the NBA finals. This year his contract was up for grabs. On July 8, in an overwrought, live prime-time ESPN special that seemed to offend nearly every sports fan in America, James declared he would be joining the Miami Heat. Suffice it to say: there was no joy in Cleveland.

Basketball

Hoosier Daddy, Butler?

Fish gotta swim, birds gotta fly—and Duke University's Blue Devils, it seems, just gotta win the NCAA basketball championship every year or two. In 2010, Coach Mike Krzyzewski's Blue Devils did it again, winning their fourth national title in Indianapolis by beating Butler University, hometown heroes in Indy. The usual suspects, Connecticut, won the NCAA women's crown.

Baseball
Mound Phenom Sidelined

Stephen Strasburg, a flame-throwing right-hander from California, was signed by the Washington Nationals in 2009 and handed a $15 million contract—$5 million more than any rookie player before him. In his first game, against the Pittsburgh Pirates on June 8, he struck out 14 batters. But in August the Nationals said that Strasburg had suffered an injury to his pitching arm and had undergone Tommy John surgery that will keep him out of action for 12 to 18 months.

Roller Derby
Bad Girls on Skates

We will leave it to the sociologists to explain the resurgence of women's roller derby, a game that last was popular in the 1930s, amid an earlier economic downturn. The contact sport is exploding in popularity, with players and spectators saying they love the derby's mash-up of fast action, burlesque getups and campy, tongue-in-cheek humor. Among current New York City teams: the Brooklyn Bombshells and Queens of Pain.

Errors
Year of the Bad Call

Umpires, referees and line judges are only human, and we've long been told that their very fallibility adds a uniquely uncertain and thus valuable element to our sports and games. But in an age that allows for fast video review and sensor devices to record goals, calls for deploying such technologies ratcheted up in 2010, following a spate of very bad, very public, decisions by the judges of sport.

PERFECTION DENIED

Armando Galarraga of the Detroit Tigers retired 26 Cleveland Indians in a row on June 2—but with two outs in the ninth inning, first-base umpire Jim Joyce, a respected veteran, called Jason Donald safe on an infield grounder. Joyce was wrong and quickly admitted it, but the bad call stood. At left, Joyce repents the following day, when a classy Gallaraga, 28, who publicly forgave him, brought Detroit's lineup card to the plate.

WORLD CUP FOLLIES

The World Cup, soccer's greatest stage, was tainted by a host of poor calls, many of them shown to be false in replay. At right, U.S. player Michael Bradley berates referee Koman Coulibaly of Mali after the ref denied the U.S. a clear goal against Slovenia in the 85th minute of the game.

DUSTIN JOHNSON'S BAD DAY

The pro golfer wasn't the victim of a bad call—just a very harsh one. Aiming for a three-way tie for the lead of the PGA Tournament on the last hole of the final round, Johnson grounded his club in a bunker, a deed he thought was legal. Fined two strokes, he finished tied for fifth place. At left, a PGA official delivers the bad news.

JIM FURYK'S BAD MORNING

The call that was blown in this case was Furyk's wake-up call. One of the PGA's top golfers was disqualified from The Barclays tourney in August when his cell phone, which he uses as an alarm clock, ran out of power and Furyk snoozed through his scheduled 7:30 a.m. tee time.

Arts

Paradise *Lost*

Fans of the hit ABC series *Lost* came together, appropriately enough, on Waikiki Beach in Honolulu on May 23 to watch the final episode of what TIME TV critic James Poniewozik called the tube's "biggest, head-trippiest, desert-island adventure." Count Poniewozik among the fans: anticipating the finale of the series, which ran for six seasons, he wrote, "In an era of diminished major-network expectations, *Lost* has made big, demanding, intellectual TV on a broadcast network." The final airing, a double episode, ran for 150 min. and attracted an audience of some 13.5 million viewers; 20.7 million had tuned in to watch the final episode of the series' first season, in 2004-05.

Na'vi *Zoe Saldana played Neytiri, the film's heroine. Her performance was filmed using powerful new motion-capture technology, then digitally altered to create her alien features*

At Last, Movies With More Depth

Well, visual depth, anyway. James Cameron's trailblazing blockbuster *Avatar* ignites a new era of 3-D films in Hollywood

THE LAST SHOT OF *AVATAR* IS A CLOSE-UP OF A character's closed eyes snapping open. That was the climax and the message of James Cameron's first fiction feature since his 1997 smash, *Titanic:* Look around! Embrace the movie—surely the most vivid and convincing creation of a fantasy world ever seen in the history of moving pictures—as a total sensory, sensuous, sensual experience. The planet Pandora that Cameron and his army of artist-technicians created, at a budget believed to be in excess of $300 million, is a wonder world of flora and fauna: a rain forest (where it hardly ever rains) of gigantic trees and phosphorescent plants, of six-legged flying horses, panther

dogs and hammerhead dinosaurs. Living among these creatures is Pandora's humanish tribe, the Na'vi, a lean, 10-ft.-tall, blue-striped people with yellow eyes—or what mankind might have been if it had evolved in harmony with, and not in opposition to, the Edenic environment that gave rise to its birth.

Count TIME critic Richard Corliss among those bedazzled by Cameron's new world. "*Avatar* is a state-of-the-art experience that for years to come will define what movies can achieve, not in duplicating our existence but in confecting new ones," he wrote. "The story may be familiar from countless old movies, from those made in Hollywood like *Dances with Wolves* (an American grows sympathetic to the tribes he was meant to annihilate) and *Apocalypse Now* (and any number of anti-imperialist war epics) to those made abroad, like 2009's *District 9* (set in South Africa, where a human becomes part-alien and is hunted down by his old own kind). Some of the dialogue in *Avatar's* opening sequences may be on the starchy side —Cameron has never been a great director of actors nor sympathetic to their sensitive needs—but objections shrink to quibbles and then simply disappear in the face of the picture's unprecedented visual flourishes."

Audiences were just as impressed. *Avatar* opened on Dec. 18, 2009, in time for the holiday movie crowds, and through the first months of 2010 the movie was a mainstay at the nation's multiplexes. It was No. 1 at the box office for seven weeks straight in the U.S. and Canada, and by February it had surpassed *Titanic* to become the highest-grossing film in Hollywood history, and the first to take in more than $2 billion worldwide.

Cameron's film broke so much new technical ground that it will take years for filmmakers to absorb all his innovations. The live-action filming was created with the proprietary digital Fusion 3-D Camera System, developed by Cameron and colleague Vince Pace. The *Avatar* team also developed a new and far more powerful version of the motion-capture technology familiar from the character of Gollum in *The Lord of the Rings* trilogy. The final film, Cameron estimated, consists of 60% computer-generated scenes and 40% live-action scenes.

In Hollywood *Avatar's* success was attributed to its snazzy 3-D look, setting off a frenzy that rivaled the development of CinemaScope in the 1950s. New 3-D epics were given the green light, and even films already shot and currently in postproduction were taken back to the lab to be given a 3-D make-over. Cameron and *Avatar* had managed to open up the eyes of even the most jaded of viewers: movie studio executives. ∎

Fabulist *Cameron, at the console, shows footage to stars Sigourney Weaver, left, Joel Moore and Sam Worthington*

IN BRIEF

Multiplex Memories.
Geeky boys, more toys and dreamy ploys

THE SOCIAL NETWORK
The film about the creation of Facebook, for all its 21st century interests, is connected to social dramas from the 1970s: fact-based films that created severely flawed protagonists and addressed big, contemporary themes, never stopping to worry about the youth market or the Hollywood edict of a happy ending. The film is like a video game at warp speed, but for the ear-brain instead of the eye-hand ... its rewards are mammoth and exhilarating. —*By Richard Corliss*

TOY STORY 3

Pixar filmmakers have to be able to tap into their vestigial child. In that sense, the *Toy Story* series is their collective autobiography. The Pixarians—from creative director John Lasseter on down—are smart kids who never renounced their childish belief that anything is possible. Why, to make an instant classic like *Toy Story 3*, it just takes an unfettered imagination, several hundred artists and technicians, about $200 million and four years of nonstop work. Child's play. —*R.C.*

INCEPTION
Writer-director Christopher Nolan's first movie since *The Dark Knight* is a story about dreams—our most intimate intellectual property—and about how they may not be safe from theft. This is a film more to admire than to cherish, one that aims to fascinate rather than to satisfy familiar impulses. It's a beautiful object, like a perpetually spinning top, not a living organism. This is a movie that you will wish you had crammed for. —*R.C.*

Show Stoppers. Punk rock takes Broadway, Pacino takes a gondola, and Swift takes a batch of Grammys

Taylor Swift

The country-pop star isn't even old enough to drink yet, but she continued her reign atop the music charts, picking up four Grammy Awards, including Album of the Year for her 2009 smash *Fearless.* And she was still milking the sympathy she received when rapper Kanye West grabbed her microphone to diss her award for Best Female Video at the 2009 MTV Music Video Awards. Her response arrived in the form of an acoustic ballad, *Innocent.* Was Swift forgiving her loudmouthed heckler? The lyrics "Who you are is not what you did" seem to convey graceful compassion. But then she calls West "32 and still growing up." Unlike herself—20 and all grown up.

Arcade Fire

The increasingly popular group from Montreal, led by Win Butler, center, and wife Régine Chassagne, left, released its third album, *The Suburbs*, which charmed critics and became their first No. 1 album in the U.S. upon its release in August. Said TIME: "Arcade Fire can't parallel-park without writing an anthemic suite about it. Their third album's lush bombast underscores its articulate compassion for sad suburban kids who grow into crushed adults."

Broken Bells

"You may not have heard of Broken Bells yet," TIME's Claire Suddath wrote in March, "but you probably know the band's members. Musician-producer Danger Mouse [Brian Burton]—one-half of Gnarls Barkley and the genius behind *The Grey Album*, the Beatles/Jay-Z mashup— has teamed up with the Shins' lead singer, James Mercer, to create a new band, a new sound and a new album." The band— that's Mercer at left and DM in center— clicked, and the album became a hit.

Sade

The exotic world-beat star with a famously breathy delivery returned to the charts after a long absence. Said TIME: "After a decade of silence, what's new and differ- ent about Sade? Nothing—and that's good news. *Soldier of Love* spins the same hip, sinuous mix that cast a spell over the 1980s and '90s. Her alto is a little huskier, her songs a little darker, but she's still a supremely smooth operator."

THE YEAR IN THEATER

American Idiot

Broadway has embraced rock operas and jukebox musicals loosely assembled from old pop hits. In 2010 it finally went punk with *American Idiot*, based on the 2004 concept album by Oakland, Calif., band Green Day. TIME critic Richard Zoglin loved the music, but found the book lacking: "Where the show falls short is as a fully developed narrative."

The Addams Family

The characters are beloved from the *New Yorker* and old TV and movie hits. The stars were aligned: Bebe Neuwirth and Nathan Lane. Audiences liked it, but the show won no Tonys—we'll blame composer Andrew Lippa and writers Marshall Brickman and Rick Elice.

The Merchant of Venice

When Al Pacino starred as Shylock in a film version of Shakespeare's *The Merchant of Venice* in 2005, TIME movie critic Richard Corliss admired the star's restraint: "Though he has a few oratorical geysers, he mostly understates his venom. Pacino seems to recall, from his early Michael Corleone days, the power of whis- pered menace." In 2010 Pacino again played Shylock, this time in an outdoor staging in New York City's Central Park. Pacino chewed a bit more scenery, critics noted, but he was so effective that the show transferred to Broadway in October.

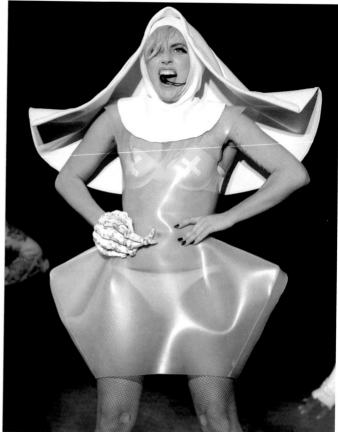

PROFILE

Lady Gaga

She dances, she prances, she takes political stances.
And the Empress of Pop is definitely wearing new clothes

IT WORKED FOR SAMUEL CLEMENS. IT DID WONDERS for Robert Zimmerman. And the quintessentially American ploy of reinventing one's sorry self as the glittering person one would prefer to be still has lots to offer, it seems. Consider the case of Stefani Joanne Angelina Germanotta, who as of 2007 was only another former Catholic high school girl seeking to make a name for herself in the music business in New York City. But she couldn't seem to break through until she actually did make a name for herself: she adopted the moniker Lady Gaga as an echo of the single *Radio Ga Ga*, a 1984 European hit for British glam rockers Queen. With her new alter ego succinctly encapsulating her mission statement, Stefani was ready to join the likes of Mark Twain and Bob Dylan as American icons.

Today, at only 24, Lady Gaga reigns over an empire of admirers. She rules the pop charts with hits like *Poker Face* (2008) and *Bad Romance* (2009), which are dance-floor friendly, if not exactly innovative. She is the toast of the fashion world, as she parades around stages sporting a succession of outré costumes carefully calibrated to evoke shock and awe. The media sit at her feet, for she provides bloggers, paparazzi and editors with the 21st century equivalent of "good copy." And, in a more serious vein, she is a respected and hard-working activist who has addressed rallies from Washington to Maine on behalf of gay rights.

Now and then, however, Gaga can be accused of mixing her metaphors. Shortly after she wore an outfit apparently composed of cuts of meat at the 2010 MTV Video Music Awards—where she picked up a six-pack of statues— she told a crowd at an anti–"Don't ask, don't tell" rally, "Equality is the prime rib of America, but because I'm gay I don't get to enjoy the greatest cut of meat my country has to offer."

116

Curiouser and curiouser *Among the outfits Lady Gaga has sported in her failed attempts to elude the spotlight: from left, a sheath of meat; a see-through nun; and, well, insert your guess here*

Whatever. But in 2010, the formerly pitch-perfect pop star stumbled once or twice. In the summer, she showed up at both Yankee Stadium and the Met's Citi Field park. At the first she threw hissy fits when banished from the dressing rooms; at the second, she flipped the bird at cameras. On the Lollapalooza tour, a trashed Gaga foresook high fashion to try crowd-surfing; her stab at abandonment evoked misery rather than Mizrahi.

Earth to Gaga: a new incarnation of the spirit of Freddy Mercury, David Bowie and Madonna is always welcome. But one Courtney Love is surely more than enough. ∎

Jonathan Franzen

Like the great Victorian novelists, he shows us the way we live now

HE IS A MEMBER OF AN ENDANGERED SPECIES, THE AMERICAN literary novelist, and Jonathan Franzen is uneasy about his plight. He's a physically solid guy, 6 ft. 2 in., with significant shoulders, but his posture is not so much hunched as flinched. At 51, he isn't the richest or most famous living U.S. novelist, but he is one of the most ambitious and one of the best. His third book, *The Corrections* (2001), was the literary phenomenon of the decade. His fourth novel, *Freedom*, was published in August 2010. Like *The Corrections*, it's the story of an American family, told with extraordinary power and richness.

In a lot of ways, *Freedom* looks more like a 19th century novel than a 21st century one. The trend in fiction over the past decade has been toward the closeup, the miniature, the micro-cosm. After the literary megafauna of the 1990s—like David Foster Wallace's *Infinite Jest* and Don DeLillo's *Underworld*—the novels of the aughts zoomed in deep, exploring subcultures, individual voices, specific ethnic communities.

Franzen skipped that trend. He remains a devotee of the wide shot, the all embracing, way-we-live-now novel. In that sense he's a throwback, practically a Victorian. *Freedom* isn't about a subculture; it's about the culture. It's not a microcosm; it's a cosm. *Freedom* is not the kind of Great American Novel that Franzen's predecessors crafted—not the kind Bellow and Mailer and Updike wrote. The American scene is just too complex—and too aware of its own complexity, for anything to loom that large over it ever again. But *Freedom* is big in a different way: it doesn't back down from the complexity; it encompasses it. ∎

Franzen *He brings the sweep of Dickens to a plugged-in, complex age*

117

In Brief

Spectacles

CIRQUE DU MEMPHIS *Montreal's Cirque du Soleil creates larger-than-life shows that are a perfect fit for gaudy Las Vegas. Cirque has tackled the Fab Four and Michael Jackson is on deck, but it was Elvis Presley's turn in 2010. Said* TIME's *Richard Corliss: "... The Beatles homage ... was sedate stuff next to this audiovisual-balletic-acrobatic explosion from director Vincent Paterson and 'director of creation' Armand Thomas. They've concocted an experience that's both symphonic and in every way fantastic. This is hagiography, not biography; it's no warts, all wonder."*

Books

Larsson and Lisbeth

It was another banner year for Lisbeth Salander, the punked-out, bisexual computer hacker who's the central character of the smash *Millennium Trilogy* of thrillers written by Swedish journalist Stieg Larsson before his sudden death at age 50 in 2004. The eagerly awaited third novel, *The Girl Who Kicked the Hornet's Nest*, was published in the U.S. on May 25 at No. 1 on the best-seller lists, where it remained for weeks.

The Swedish film version of the book,

starring the icy Noomi Rapace as Salander, left, was released in Scandinavia late in 2009 and was a hit across Europe in 2010. A U.S. film version of the trilogy is now under way; Rooney Mara *(The Social Network)* will play Salander. One mystery remains: Who will be awarded the rights to a fourth, partially completed novel that resides in Larsson's computer? His former partner and his family are battling it out to control Lisbeth Salander's destiny.

Television

Bryan Cranston Gets a Break

Tired of reality TV? Mad at *Mad Men?* TIME critic James Poniewozik calls AMC's *Breaking Bad* TV's top thriller, and Emmy Award voters handed the nod for Best Actor in a Drama to star Bryan Cranston the third year in a row for his depiction of Walter White, whose costly battle with terminal cancer leads him to enter the meth trade.

Poniewozik admired the show's "small moments, slowed, probed and stretched for tension. Cranston plays White haunted and emotionally taut as a guitar string. [Creator Vince] Gilligan and cinematographer Michael Slovis build that atmosphere with some of the most stylized visuals on TV."

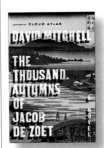

Television

Jane Lynch: Best in Show

After years of acting in commercials, minor films and TV shows, Jane Lynch, 50, caught a break as a lesbian poodle trainer in Christopher Guest's 2000 mockumentary *Best in Show*. In 2009 she excelled as Julia Child's sister in *Julie and Julia*. Now she's the toast of TV in a tart role as a hard-driving gym teacher on Fox TV's sing-along hit *Glee*—and she's got a 2010 Emmy to prove it.

Television

Simon Says: Wave Goodbye

Fox TV's hit *American Idol* has been slipping in the ratings of late, but it's still on top. The show will be tested in 2011, when its icon, tough-love judge Simon Cowell, bows out, along with Ellen DeGeneres and Kara DioGuardi. The new recruits: Aerosmith front man Steven Tyler and pop star Jennifer Lopez, below, with longtime judge Randy Jackson and host Ryan Seacrest.

Transition

Conan Redux

"*Conan*. Simple. Pure. Like the man himself." That's how TV funnyman Conan O'Brien announced the name of his new late-night show that began airing on TBS Nov. 8. The show's debut may help calm the crazed atmosphere in TV's late-night world, which saw O'Brien become a kind of folk hero after he was unceremoniously dumped from his post as host of NBC's *The Tonight Show* in late January, after former host Jay Leno's prime-time show foundered and NBC execs, unhappy with O'Brien's ratings, brought Leno back.

O'Brien got his revenge by taking his show on the road, performing live on what he dubbed the *Legally Prohibited from Being Funny on Television Tour*. And he got the last laugh when NBC boss Jeff Zucker, the man behind O'Brien's removal, said in October that he'd be leaving his job.

Books

Required Reading

TIME's critics weigh in with their choices of the year's best fiction.

THE THOUSAND AUTUMNS OF JACOB DE ZOET

David Mitchell's books seem to issue from some high-energy literary laboratory where exotic narrative configurations are tested and optimized for maximum expressive power. This novel takes place mostly on a fascinating little scrap of earth called Dejima, a walled, man-made island in Nagasaki harbor, a hothouse of capitalism and corruption crowded with castaways, conscripts, half-castes and ambitious, unscrupulous Dutchmen. —*Lev Grossman*

A VISIT FROM THE GOON SQUAD

Jennifer Egan, author of *The Keep* and *Emerald City*, returns with a genre-twisting, time-traveling tale of three generations of rock stars, including a preteen from the future who prefers to communicate via PowerPoint.—*L.G.*

SOLAR

Ian McEwan has turned his sharp, satirical eye to climate change, and the result is anything but heroic. In making *Solar* a comedy—albeit one as black as the dark side of the moon—McEwan gives the lie to vain hopes that the planet will be saved by a sudden outbreak of environmental virtue. Where *Solar* really succeeds—beyond the dark comedy, too long missing in McEwan's gentler recent work—is the author's ability to reveal the nature of the climate conundrum in the very human life of his protagonist. —*Bryan Walsh*

Milestones

Last Full Measure

Fellow soldiers salute as a coffin containing the body of U.S. Army Sergeant Joshua Lengstorf, 24, of Yoncalla, Ore., is taken from a C-17 cargo plane on Jan. 4, 2010, at Dover Air Force Base in Delaware. Lengstorf and two other U.S. soldiers were killed in a roadside bombing while serving in Operation Enduring Freedom in Afghanistan. The Bush Administration refused to permit photographers access to such moments, but the Obama Administration has allowed such photos.

Chanteuse *Lena Horne, then 25, performs for an all-white audience at the Savoy-Plaza Hotel in New York City in 1942*

Lena Horne

She weathered the storms of racism to earn a nation's respect

SHE MIGHT HAVE BEEN ONE OF BLACK AMERICA'S MOST appealing early ambassadors to the mainstream—an artist with perfect features and a sultry sweetness who would teach the benighted to accept the glamour and talent, the full humanity, of an oppressed minority that had so profoundly enriched the official culture. But blacks in her day were still second-class citizens, deprived of the bus seats, voting rights and career opportunities whites took for granted.

So Lena Horne, as determined as she was beautiful, went ahead and fashioned one of the 20th century's most exemplary and poignant show-business careers. Born to a middle-class family in Brooklyn, she joined the chorus line as a teenager at Harlem's famed Cotton Club, where everyone onstage was black and everyone in the audience white. At 20, she starred in the "race movie" *The Duke Is Tops,* but Hollywood didn't so much demean her as ignore her.

After a decade in the film desert, Horne came home to wow Broadway in the 1957 production *Jamaica.* She went on to further triumphs on Broadway, TV and the concert stage, as well as on some 40 albums and occasionally in movies. A thrilling voice for civil rights, she refused to perform before segregated audiences on World War II tours; she collaborated with Eleanor Roosevelt in winning anti-lynching legislation; and she marched with Medgar Evers in Mississippi and Martin Luther King Jr. in Washington.

Gradually, America got it. In 1981 she was back on Broadway in the one-woman show *Lena Horne: The Lady and Her Music,* telling her story, singing *Stormy Weather* and winning two Tony Awards. Long before her death, on May 9 at 92, she had become a beacon for black artists, a divinity to audiences of all colors and a lingering, stinging reproach to the attitudes that had robbed her of her Hollywood prime. ■

George Steinbrenner

Love him or hate him, he put the New York Yankees on top again

IN 1973, GEORGE STEINBRENNER, THEN THE NEW principal owner of the New York Yankees, uttered one of the most comically inaccurate forecasts in sports history. "We plan absentee ownership as far as running the Yankees is concerned," he told the assembled media at his introductory press conference after buying the then woeful Yankees from CBS for $8.8 million. From that moment, Steinbrenner, who died on July 13 at age 80, would become the most nonabsentee owner in the history of sport. His hundreds of impulsive hiring and firings and free-agent signings highlighted a career of meddling that got him temporarily banned from baseball, memorably spoofed on *Seinfeld*—it even earned him a hosting gig on *Saturday Night Live* playing a cartoon version of himself. But under his "absentee" reign, the Yankees won seven World Series titles and firmly established themselves as the Tiffany sports team in this country. Today his club is worth some $1.6 billion—quite a return on investment.

Was Steinbrenner good for baseball? That question will be endlessly analyzed as time passes. If you're a player—or a Yankees fan—the answer is an easy yes. Once baseball's reserve clause was lifted in the 1970s and the free-agency era began, it was the Boss who opened up his checkbook, bringing stars like Reggie Jackson, Catfish Hunter and Dave Winfield to the Bronx. No one would outspend the Yankees, and every overpaid player in baseball today should hand over some commission to Steinbrenner's estate.

Steinbrenner's truculent, the-Boss-is-always-right style created epic clashes with his managers and players, not the least of which was with Billy Martin, whom he dumped as manager five times. He even alienated the sainted Yogi Berra, although the two repaired their relationship in later years.

Not everyone was as forgiving of Steinbrenner as Yogi. In 1990, baseball commissioner Fay Vincent banned Steinbrenner from baseball for life because he had paid a known gambler to dig up dirt on Winfield, who by the end of his Yankee days was feuding with the owner, like so many others before him. It was Steinbrenner's second baseball

suspension: in the 1970s, he pleaded guilty to making illegal campaign contributions to Richard Nixon's re-election fund. That two-year penalty was reduced to 15 months, and in 1989 President Ronald Reagan pardoned Steinbrenner.

The Boss was too complex to be defined by his payroll. He'd needlessly berate a hapless team employee one minute, then quietly give money to local hospitals the next. He'd alienate a legend like Berra by firing him 16 games into a season but give second chances to drug abusers like Darryl Strawberry and Dwight Gooden. Before Steinbrenner, sports owners were a relatively buttoned-up, civic-minded lot. Now they all seem to be bombastic, just like the Boss. For better and for worse, George Steinbrenner changed baseball, and sports, forever. ∎

The Boss *Steinbrenner takes in a spring-training game in 1996*

Slow learner *Hopper was wed five times. His briefest marriage was an eight-day whirlwind with the Mamas and the Papas' Michelle Phillips. "The first seven," he said, "were pretty good"*

Dennis Hopper

The rebel actor's ride was exhilarating, but few would call it easy

IN HOLLYWOOD, A TOWN THAT PROVIDED A LOT OF competition among perpetrators of shenanigans, he was one of the foremost cokies, alkies, crazies. At a Houston-area art event in the early 1980s, he nearly blew himself up with 17 sticks of dynamite. Given that for a couple of decades he seemed bent on killing himself for pleasure's sake, it's a wonder that Dennis Hopper had such a long success in movies— more than 50 years—and so many other pursuits. When he died on May 29 at 74, he was remembered not only as an actor but also as a director, a noted photographer and an art collector with a fine eye.

When your first movie role is as "Goon" in *Rebel Without a Cause*, tormenting James Dean, with whom you become close friends ... and, when you're 22, your Method misbehavior so exasperates old-line director Henry Hathaway that he blackballs you from feature-film work for seven years ... and when

Easy Rider, the little movie you directed, co-wrote and starred in, makes a bundle and becomes the definitive fracture point in the Hollywood studio system ... and when your next directorial effort, *The Last Movie,* is taken as a bird-flip to the industry and crashes like the *Hindenburg* ... when, in your later roles, you're the least stable character in some very strange and wonderful films, out-nutsying Marlon Brando in *Apocalypse Now* and Isabella Rossellini in *Blue Velvet* ... and when you are found naked and raving with cocaine psychosis in the Mexican jungle ... then, even if you're a teetotaler and a Republican (both of which Hopper became in the mid-'80s), you will attract attention.

Despite his myriad self-inflicted wounds, the middle-class kid from Dodge City, Kansas, somehow survived, and thrived, until his last, most unlikely role: as one of Hollywood's elder statesmen. ∎

Louise Bourgeois

Late in her life, the world caught up with her disturbing visions

THOUGH SHE WORKED FOR DECADES IN RELATIVE obscurity, the French-born American artist Louise Bourgeois, who died May 31 at 98, was the ultimate insider. With wit, courage and a bewitching perversity, she tunneled deep inside both the body and the psyche and returned with work of surpassing and hypnotic strangeness. Wood, marble, latex, wax and bronze were her materials. So were anxiety, anger, bitter memory and a longing for refuge.

Born in 1911, she grew up in Choisy-le-Roi, where her parents ran a tapestry workshop. Her father's many extramarital affairs—including a long involvement with her governess—left her with a lifetime of resentment that she channeled into her art. In 1938 she married an American art historian, moved to New York and began exhibiting. But it wasn't until 1982 that she became abruptly famous with a retrospective at the Museum of Modern Art in New York

City, the first there for any woman artist, that proved she was not only a brilliant inheritor of the surrealist tradition but also a feminist pioneer. Ahead of her was some of her most widely seen work, like the ambivalent homage to her mother called *Maman*—a giant spider exhibited around the world. She roared into her 70s as the insider who finally broke out.

Reviewing Bourgeois' breakthrough 1982 show, TIME art critic Robert Hughes observed, "What Bourgeois sets up is a totemic, surrealistic imagery of weak threats, defenses, lairs, wombs, almost inchoate groupings of form. Her work is by turns aggressive and pathetic, sexually charged and physically awkward, tense and shapeless. It employs an imagery of encounter to render concrete an almost inescapable sense of solitude. In short, it is physically, if not always formally, rich stuff." And the world of art was the richer for it. ∎

Oedipal vision? *At left is Bourgeois in 1996, when she was 84; she received her first major show in 1982, at age 70. Above, one of her best-known works, a 29-ft. (9 m) sculpture of a spider, lurks outside the Guggenheim Museum Bilbao in Spain*

Early Byrd *The Senator during his 1964 filibuster opposing the Civil Rights bill. An authority on the Senate, Byrd wrote a well-received four-volume history of the institution in partnership with the chamber's in-house historian*

Robert C. Byrd

He embodied the U.S. Senate, West Virginia—and federal largesse

FOR MORE THAN A THIRD OF ITS 144-YEAR EXISTENCE, the state of West Virginia was represented in the U.S. Senate by one man: Robert C. Byrd. So encompassing was his 50 years of service in the Senate and so encyclopedic was his institutional knowledge that by the time he died at 92 on June 28, he had become not just the political personification of West Virginia in the nation's capital but also the embodiment of the Senate to the rest of the country. Twice its majority leader and a master of its all-powerful rules, Byrd was as much a part of the place as the wooden desks, steep-sloped galleries and soaring speeches that filled it.

Raised by impoverished coal-mining relatives in Depression-era Appalachia after his mother died in the 1918 influenza pandemic, Byrd showed an early gift for two things: self-education and rhetorical charm. The latter skill more than the former paved the way for his election, first to the statehouse as a

Democrat in 1946, then to the U.S. House of Representatives in 1952 and finally to the Senate in 1958.

In the 1952 race, his opponent revealed that Byrd had belonged to the Ku Klux Klan in the early '40s. Byrd quickly dismissed the membership as a "mistake of youth." He later helped filibuster what would become the Civil Rights Act of 1964, giving a near record 14-hour speech, and he opposed the 1965 voting-rights bill. After ousting Ted Kennedy as Democratic whip in 1971, he moderated his positions in line with the party's mainstream. Having supported the military buildup in Vietnam, by 2003 he was among the most outspoken Senators against the invasion of Iraq.

If Byrd's political positions changed over the years, his dedication to lavish government spending never did. It was his ability to send federal funds to West Virginia that led to huge victory pluralities late in his career—when he faced any opposition at all. ∎

J.D. Salinger

A single novel won him enduring fame—which he detested

TAKE THE AUSTERE LITTLE PAPERBACKS DOWN FROM the shelf, and you can hold the collected works of J.D. Salinger—one novel, three volumes of stories—in the palm of one hand. Like some of his favorite writers—Sappho, for example, whom we know only from ancient fragments, or the Japanese poets who crafted 17-syllable haiku—Salinger was an author whose large reputation pivots on very little. The first of his published stories that he thought were good enough to preserve appeared in the *New Yorker* in 1948. Seventeen years later, he placed one last story there and drew down the shades.

From that day until his death on Jan. 27 at age 91, at his home in Cornish, N.H., Salinger was the hermit crab of American letters. When he emerged, it was usually to complain that somebody was poking at his shell. Over time Salinger's exemplary refusal of his own fame may turn out to be as important as his fiction. In the 1960s he retreated to the small house in Cornish and rejected the idea of being a public figure. Thomas Pynchon is his obvious successor in that department. But Pynchon figured out how to turn his back on the world with a wink and a Cheshire Cat smile. Salinger did it with a scowl. Then again, he was inventing the idea, and he bent over it with an inventor's sweaty intensity.

Salinger's only novel, *The Catcher in the Rye*, was published in 1951 and gradually achieved a status that made him cringe. For decades the book was a universal rite of passage for adolescents, the manifesto of disenchanted youth. Holden Caulfield, its petulant, yearning (and arguably manic-depressive) young hero, was the original angry young man.

Born in New York City to a Scots-born Protestant mother and a Jewish father who was a food importer, Salinger was an underachieving student who ran through a succession of schools and dropped out of New York University after two semesters. He finally decided he wanted to be a writer, and he succeeded: his stories were published in mass-market magazines like *Collier's* and *Esquire* before he was drafted to serve in World War II, where he landed at Normandy on D-day, fought in hellish conditions in northern Europe—and may have suffered a nervous breakdown. Once back in New York City, he forged a relationship with the *New Yorker*, which would publish all his remaining short stories and novellas.

Much of Salinger's later work is devoted to his chronicles of the Glass family, an intricate hybrid of show biz and spirituality. Many critics suggest that the Glasses make up a kind of group portrait of Salinger, each of them a reflection of his different dimensions: the writer and the actor, the searcher and the researcher, the spiritual adept and the prat-falling schmuck. That may very well be true. He made sure we could never be sure. Holden Caulfield says, "Don't ever tell anybody anything." That's one time you know it's Salinger talking. He struggled all his long life with the contradiction between his gifts as a writer and his impulse to refuse them. ■

Do not disturb *This photo of the reclusive author is from 1951*

Alexander McQueen

THE WORK OF DESIGNER ALEXANDER-McQueen, who took his life at age 40 on Feb. 11, was spectacular. It was never sloppy, lazy or cavalier. It was magnificently and precisely what he wanted. His work was whimsical and full of humor; it was subversive, political and incredibly sexual. Sometimes it was beautifully ugly, and that was brave. He carried the torch for a new generation.

—By Sarah Jessica Parker, actress and chief creative director of Halston

Patricia Neal

THE BRILLIANT HOLLYWOOD STAR WOULD NEVER HAVE BEEN CAST TO play herself in *The Patricia Neal Story.* Her screen persona, in movies like *The Fountainhead* and *Breakfast at Tiffany's,* was one of elegance and hauteur. Even when the ice goddess thawed, as she did in her portrayal of Paul Newman's earthy housekeeper in *Hud,* which won her an Academy Award for Best Actress in 1964, Neal gave an edge to all those curves; here was a woman no man would easily mess with.

Offscreen, the Knoxville, Tenn., native radiated a warm Southern gentility rarely seen in her movies. And in real life, especially over a few years in the 1960s, the actress who dished it out had to be the woman and mother who could take it. She endured a series of calamities: the brain damage her 4-month-old son Theo suffered when his carriage was crushed by a taxi, the death of her 7-year-old daughter Olivia after a bout of measles, and the three massive strokes one night in 1965 that left the pregnant Neal in a coma for three weeks and required years of therapy for her to be able to speak, walk and act again.

No performer wants to be the star of her own tragedy; but Neal, who died at 84 on Aug. 8, proved herself a towering figure who rebounded from all her ordeals. Few actresses can say their career was an inspiration, fewer still that their life was a tragedy with a triumphant ending. In her drawling, seductive voice, Patricia Neal could say both.

Alexander Haig

WHEREVER HE SERVED, HE MADE A DIFference. I recruited Alexander Haig, who died on Feb. 20 at age 85, for the National Security Council staff as my deputy. One

of his principal tasks was to help end a war that President Richard Nixon had inherited and in which Al had fought. It proved a heartrending journey, especially for a soldier. But with typical skill and dedication, Al extricated America from war while preserving the nation's honor.

—By Henry Kissinger, former National Security Adviser and Secretary of State

John Wooden

MAYBE VINCE LOMBARDI WAS MORE MAJESTIC AND RED AUERBACH A MORE colorful figure. But John Wooden, the former UCLA basketball coach who died at 99 on June 4, could lay claim to his own honorific. No great coach in history was more beloved, and no beloved coach greater, than the Wizard of Westwood. At UCLA, Wooden won 10 national basketball championships, a run that included seven straight titles from 1967 to 1973. But despite the outlandish numbers, Wooden's character transcended his accomplishments. "Your heart must be in your work," he wrote—from experience.

Charles Moore

IF GREAT PHOTOJOURNALISTS KNOW WHERE TO STAND, CHARLES MOORE KNEW where to be. He was there in all the right places of our civil rights imagination. This small, wiry white Southerner, who died March 9 at 79, had his lens, and his courage, at the ready: in Birmingham, Ala., in 1963, for example, when Bull Connor's water cannons pounded men and women seeking only an equal opportunity. Charles Moore was an unassuming man with a softly charged voice who probably didn't weigh 140 lbs. But even when he was in his mid-70s, you could see the old Golden Gloves boxer and ex-Marine who'd refused to back down. He once modestly said about his work, which he

wouldn't have called art, although it unquestionably was, "I project myself into a person. I look at everything, the arms, the hands, the expression. I wait for the moment ... I shoot." As if that were all it took.

—*By Paul Hendrickson, author of* Sons of Mississippi: A Story of Race and Its Legacy

Tony Curtis

THE MOVIE STAR, WHO DIED ON Sept. 29 at 85 of cardiac arrest, was born Bernard Schwartz in the Bronx in 1925. He found his first great movie role in 1957's *Sweet Smell of Success* as Sidney Falco, the slick nogoodnik par excellence, a pretty boy on the make—all hustle, no morals, and with a line of patter like petty larceny. Then, two years later, he was cast as a stud saxophone player, with Jack Lemmon as his partner and Marilyn Monroe as the bait, in Billy Wilder's *Some Like It Hot.* Tony Curtis got the best of everything: two all-time classics, two defining roles.

As Eddie Fisher was to the pop music of the early 1950s, Curtis was to that period's movies: a handsome Jewish prince for American girls to fall in love with. Like Fisher, Curtis also found a Gentile princess: in 1951 he married actress Janet Leigh, she of the sensible freshness and intoxicating allure; they had two children. After they divorced, he married five more times and fathered four more children. For 50 years after his glory days, Curtis plied his craft, appearing on TV shows and in minor films.

Mitch Miller

THE GOATEED BANDLEADER, WHO HOSTED NBC'S *SING ALONG WITH Mitch* in the early 1960s, died July 31 at age 99. When the show debuted in 1961, Miller—originally an oboe player—was already a music impresario, having produced hits for Tony Bennett and Rosemary Clooney, among others, and he's recognized as one of the first to employ overdubbing, layering different tracks in the studio. As a musician, he'd played with George Gershwin and recorded with Charlie Parker. His own *Sing Along* albums led to his TV show, which featured performances of wholesome songs with onscreen lyrics to allow the home audience to join in. Even as his show became popular, the growth of rock music (which Miller personally disdained) was superseding the kind of novelty songs and standards the host preferred.

Lynn Redgrave

IN A 1967 COVER STORY, *TIME* wrote that Lynn Redgrave's "eyes look out between the lashes with a wonderful sparkling sanity." The actress, who died May 2 at 67 following years of living with breast cancer, never lost that vivacious quality. The youngest of Sir Michael Redgrave and Rachel Kempson's three stage-struck children, she made her screen debut as a barmaid in *Tom Jones* and at 23 hit it big as the lead in *Georgy Girl*. The part of a chubby, sweet young woman out of place in the swinging '60s earned her an Oscar award for Best Actress. Over her nearly 50-year stage career, Redgrave scored multiple Tony nominations, acted with Sir Laurence Olivier and Noël Coward—and never lost that sparkle.

Harvey Pekar

HARVEY PEKAR, WHO DIED JULY 12 AT age 70, was one of a handful of veteran underground comic-book creators—including Robert Crumb, with whom he collaborated—who laid the foundation for the flourishing graphic-novel scene today. Harvey, an autodidact who could draw only stick figures, recognized that there was no intrinsic reason comic books could not explore the same human terrain as prose literature. His autobiographical stories, illustrated by a large and varied stable of cartoonists and printed in his long-running *American Splendor* series, have had an enormous influence on practitioners of the comic-book medium, and he was also a respected jazz critic.

Almost every cartoonist who writes and draws personal stories today owes a debt to Harvey's unsentimental depiction of his life and foibles, which were portrayed in a 2003 film starring Paul Giamatti. A file clerk at a Veterans Affairs hospital, Harvey may have been one of the few authentic working-class voices active in any of the arts. Harvey struggled hard for everything he got and never quite felt his struggles would let up. Along the way, he left an indelible stamp on the comic-book medium.

—By Joe Sacco, graphic artist and frequent Pekar collaborator

Malcolm McLaren

THE GADFLY AND IMPRESARIO, who died April 8 at 64, will be recalled as a master manipulator who inflicted punk on the world when he detonated the explosion that was the Sex Pistols—the most famous punk-rock group ever. A professional troublemaker by nature and a haberdasher, boutique owner and rock-'n'-roll manager by trade, Malcolm McLaren lived life more as a "glorious accident" (a term he used to describe the Pistols' Sid Vicious) than as a strategic campaign. He was more naive than he was ever credited for, except when it came to realizing how much money there was to be made. Pistols lead singer Johnny Rotten had to sue McLaren for the rights to and unpaid revenues of the Sex Pistols, winning control in 1987. McLaren went on to have successes with Adam and the Ants and Bow Wow Wow before becoming the true talent behind his own hip-hop- and opera-inspired pop tunes, as well as a dozen other songs, throughout the 1980s and '90s.
—*By Legs McNeil, co-founder of* Punk *magazine*

Bobby Thomson

ON OCT. 3, 1951, BOBBY THOMSON, THE FORMER NEW YORK GIANTS THIRD baseman who died on Aug. 16 at 86, stepped into the batter's box. It was the bottom of the ninth, and the Giants trailed the Brooklyn Dodgers 4-2, with runners on second and third. The winner would face the Yankees in the World Series. Pitcher Ralph Branca threw a fastball and—with the sport's first coast-to-coast TV audience tuned in—Thomson smacked it into the left-field stands. "The Giants win the pennant!" shouted announcer Russ Hodges five times. The Scottish-born Thomson said he received mail almost daily from people sharing their sentiments about the Shot Heard Round the World. The pennant-winning hit will forever remain the sport's most famous home run.

Art Linkletter

THE LONGTIME TV HOST, WHO DIED MAY 26 AT 97, WAS ONE OF A HANDFUL of personalities from television's early days who helped America get comfortable with the still scrappy medium. Art Linkletter was not a ham like Uncle Miltie or an innovator like Steve Allen but rather a skilled, ever self-effacing communicator who mastered the art of bringing out the foibles of ordinary folks. As host of *People Are Funny,* a reality-TV forerunner that ran from 1954 to 1961, he got audience members to participate in wild stunts without ever seeming condescending. On *House Party,* his daytime variety show that ran from 1952 to 1969, he coaxed hilarity out of children, a segment he later turned into the best-selling book *Kids Say the Darndest Things.* After his daughter's suicide in 1969, which he blamed on her LSD use, he became an antidrug crusader and right-wing hero. But his appeal was genuine and all-embracing.

Bol

Manute Bol

THE FIRST TIME I SAW [THE 7 FT. 7 in.] Manute Bol, I was like, You gotta be kidding me. We played together in a summer league. I was the smallest person to play, and he was the tallest, so it was almost like a Globetrotters show going on the road. Guys just loved him ... he was very approachable and was always playing around with people. Manute, who died June 19 at 47, had that smile and a warmness about him. He would talk about things we, as Americans, have that they don't have in Sudan ... from what I've heard, he gave all his money back to his country. It's a sad story that he had to leave us at an early age.

—By Spud Webb, who played in the NBA for 12 seasons

Tom Bosley

THERE ARE TWO TYPES OF TV DADS: those who play somebody's dad, and those who make you feel as if they could be—almost, in some way, as if they are—your dad. Tom Bosley, a TV fixture as the Cunningham clan's paterfamilias on the long-running hit *Happy Days*, was the latter. His Howard Cun-

ningham, hardware store owner and '50s dad, could be gruff and cranky—especially with his boarder Arthur Fonzarelli—but there was also something inherently fatherly and comforting about his rich voice and rumpled dignity. A stage and screen veteran (who won a Tony starring in *Fiorello!*), he was something of a father to the cast as well, as former co-stars, including Henry Winkler, remembered him. Bosley, who died on Oct. 19 at 83, also starred in the cleric-sleuth title role of *The Father Dowling Mysteries*.

Bosley

Jill Clayburgh

FOR A GENERATION OF WOMEN, Jill Clayburgh, more than any other actress, embodied a new ideal of empowerment, most notably in her 1978 triumph, *An Unmarried Woman*, in which she played a divorced woman seeking to rebuild her life; the role brought her an Oscar nomination for Best Actress.

"There was practically nothing for women to do on the screen in the 1950s and 1960s," she said in a 1978 interview. "Sure, Marilyn Monroe was great, but she had to play a one-sided character, a vulnerable sex object. It was a real fantasy."

The role of Erica Benton in *An*

Unmarried Woman was only one of many Clayburgh illuminated with her bright intellect and easy grace: she also starred in *Semi-Tough, I'm Dancing as Fast as I Can* and *Starting Over*, which brought her another Best Actress Oscar nomination.

Clayburgh's Broadway résumé included roles in Tom Stoppard's *Jumpers* and the musical *Pippin*, and she earned two Emmy Award nominations for her TV work. Before her death on Nov. 5 at 66, Clayburgh endured a 21-year battle with chronic lymphocytic leukemia that showed her real-life courage matched that of her characters.

Hank Cochran

FRIENDS CALLED NASHVILLE SONGwriter Hank Cochran "the Legend," and he earned the title with such hits as Patsy Cline's *I Fall to Pieces*, which he wrote with Harland Howard, and *Make the World Go Away*. Cochran died on July 15 at 74. Recalling his way with words in TIME, country star Larry Gatlin recounted a favorite story: "Hank was asleep in his house, where Red Lane was writing a song, which went something like 'Her love was so sweet, that I can still taste it ...' Red kept singing that over and over,

Clayburgh

Coleman

but he couldn't think of the next line. All of a sudden Hank opened his eyes and said, 'She made her mark and then erased it,' and he went back to sleep."

Gary Coleman

GARY COLEMAN, WHO DIED MAY 28 at 42, was the quintessential 1970s-80s TV kid: a figure of exaggerated childishness (in his height and chubby cheeks) with a stand-up pro's confidence and timing. As Arnold Jackson on *Diff'rent Strokes*, he was resilient and sunny, but there was a canny and suspicious element to him ("Whatchoo talkin' 'bout, Willis?") that hinted he'd been through harder times. It was a savvy comic performance for a kid who started in the role at age 10.

Coleman, who suffered from a congenital kidney disease that limited his growth, was figuratively preserved in his fans' minds as that pudgy-faced kid. But he will also be remembered for his well-publicized troubles as a former child actor, with all that signifies in American culture. "When people remember him," wrote TIME's James Poniewozik, "they will inevitably remember what he lost. But it's also

worth remembering what he had and what he gave his fans."

Jimmy Dean

HOW'S THIS FOR ECLECTIC? JIMMY Dean spent a third of his career crooning, a third acting and a third producing the namesake breakfast sausage. Born in Plainview, Texas, in 1928, Dean began his career as a radio host in Washington; he had his first hit in 1961, with *Big Bad John*, a song that earned him a Grammy and helped launch his TV career as host of *The Jimmy Dean Show* on ABC. He guest-hosted *The Tonight Show* early in Johnny Carson's run, but turned from TV to acting in the late 1960s, playing a role in the 1971 James Bond flick, *Diamonds Are Forever*. In later years he was best known for his sausage company, which he founded in 1969; he remained its pitchman through 2004, when he alleges he was pushed out because of his age. He died at 81 on June 13.

Dino De Laurentiis

THE ITALIAN FILM PRODUCER WAS the moneyman behind a mind-boggling collection of movies, ranging from important early works of Federico Fellini *(La Strada, Nights of Cabiria)* and David Lynch's 1986

Dean

masterpiece *Blue Velvet* to such mass-market favorites as *Serpico, Death Wish* and *Three Days of the Condor*. De Laurentiis, who died at 91 on Nov. 10, was a pioneer of the international co-production format in the 1950s, luring Hollywood stars Audrey Hepburn, Anthony Quinn, Henry Fonda and Kirk Douglas to Italy to star in oversized spectacles that played well worldwide. An old-fashioned

Forsythe

mogul, he married actress Silvana Mangano and founded a dynasty of Hollywood producers and celebrities, including granddaughter Giada De Laurentiis, the cable-TV chef.

John Forsythe

HE WAS THE GENIAL *BACHELOR Father*, the unseen boss of *Charlie's Angels*, the put-upon plutocrat of *Dynasty*. John Forsythe's gift as an actor was that he never made it seem like acting—he was instead the good-looking, confident, reassuring exemplar of something like American royalty. He died on April 1 at 92. "If an actor is someone who sells the script without making it sound like a carny's come-on," wrote TIME's Richard Corliss, "then John Forsythe was John Barrymore. And he did it for 60 years."

Parker

Peter Graves

JIM PHELPS HAS ACCEPTED HIS final assignment. Peter Graves, best known as the implacable leader of TV's *Mission: Impossible* team from 1967 to '73, died March 14 at 83. Thus ended a 60-year career in which his flinty features, suitable for carving on Mount Rushmore, and his sonorous baritone made him one of the small screen's leading authority figures—an eminence he occasionally subverted in irreverent comedies like *Airplane!* and *Men in Black II.* The younger brother of *Gunsmoke* star James Arness, Graves arrived in Hollywood by 1950 and got his first important role, as the all-American soldier who turns out to be a German spy in Billy Wilder's 1953 war comedy *Stalag 17.*

Penn

Throughout the '50s he alternated supporting parts in big films with leads in sci-fi anticlassics. Seemingly born middle-aged, Graves wore well, guesting on *7th Heaven* into his 80s.

Fess Parker

CHANCES ARE, IF YOU GREW UP IN the mid-1950s, you either owned an official Davy Crockett coonskin cap or had the lyrics of the television show's theme song committed to memory. Under the iconic cap—just one of the show's many merchandising tie-ins—stood Fess Parker, who died on March 18 at 85. The 6-ft. 6-in. Texas-born actor fit the rugged American frontiersman mold so well in the five Crockett episodes of ABC's *Disneyland* that

Schorr

he went on to play Daniel Boone in the 1960s NBC series of the same name. Parker starred in such movies as *Old Yeller* and *Westward Ho, the Wagons!* In later years he founded a family winery in California.

Arthur Penn

THE DIRECTOR MADE REBEL MOVIES that were in sync with their bold times and often a little ahead of the mass audience. A charter member of the Golden Age of TV drama, Arthur Penn made his mark in three different media—theater, TV and film—with his direction of William Gibson's *The Miracle Worker. Bonnie and Clyde* (1967)

was a true-crime love story told with a modernist flair: its epochally violent climax announced that Hollywood was ready to become a full-time munitions factory.

Penn's films display an ethnographer's fascination with outsiders: people whose skin is the wrong color, whose sight is too weak or hair too long, who fight to achieve celebrity or just to keep on living— or who surrender to the siren call of mortality. Over a 50-year career, Penn always invested his projects with a passionate intelligence. And when American movies needed a little revolutionizing, he was there to make it happen. He died Sept. 28, the day after his 88th birthday.

Daniel Schorr

AGGRESSIVE REPORTING PUT DANIEL Schorr on a presidential enemies list, got him investigated by Congress and cost him jobs with CBS and CNN, but his insightful analysis captured audiences for six decades. Schorr, who died on July 23 at 93, was recruited into news broadcasting by Edward R. Murrow. During Richard Nixon's presidency, Schorr won Emmys for his reporting on the Watergate scandal.

At the peak of his CBS career, Schorr obtained and passed along a leaked copy of a classified report on illegal activities by the CIA and FBI. He refused to divulge his source to congressional investigators, and the incident ended his employment at CBS. Schorr's pull-no-punches approach to the news also shortened his stint as an analyst for CNN in the '80s. But he found his true niche on National Public Radio, where for the rest of his life, he served listeners with a voice, wit and depth of experience that remain unmatched.

—By Donald A. Ritchie,
U.S. Senate Historian

Sorensen

Theodore Sorensen

HE TRAVELED THE COUNTRY WITH John F. Kennedy during the 1960 campaign, wrote J.F.K.'s unforgettable Inaugural Address and drafted the crucial letter to Nikita Khrushchev that defused the Cuban missile crisis. It was Theodore Sorensen who most elegantly gave voice to the ideals that have defined the modern Democratic Party. It's a testament to his humility that he never, privately or publicly, took credit for those things that made the 35th President an icon of the office.

After Kennedy's assassination, Sorensen, who died on Oct. 31 at 82, became keeper of his flame, shielding it from the winds of revisionism and passing it to a new generation of Democrats. It is not every man whose words echo in history. Warm, strongheaded, idealistic and funny, Sorensen deserves to be remembered.

—By Adam Sorensen, nephew of Theodore Sorensen

Ted Stevens

SENATOR TED STEVENS NEVER WORried much about making friends in Washington. "I'm a mean, miserable s.o.b.," he bragged. Stevens was a tough character, and to underscore the point, he sometimes wore an Incredible Hulk necktie on the Senate floor. Before he was killed in a plane crash Aug. 9 at 86, Stevens harnessed that tough persona in the service of a Senate career that lasted four decades.

Stevens was a titan in both Washington and Alaska, notably during his eight-year tenure as the top Republican on the Senate Appropriations Committee, a post he used to steer billions of dollars back home, to be used in such much-criticized projects as Alaska's infamous Bridge to Nowhere. But in 2008, Stevens was found guilty of corruption for failing to disclose

Stevens

$250,000 worth of gifts from a powerful Alaska businessman. His conviction was later overturned because of prosecutorial mistakes.

Gloria Stuart

THE CAMERA LOVES YOUTH, AND in the 1930s, a young Gloria Stuart provided an essential decorative element to films directed by such masters as James Whale and John Ford. She fussed over Shirley Temple in two films and starred in a *Gold Diggers* musical. Eddie Cantor made goo-goo eyes at her; Claude Rains' invisible man brought her to screams and tears. Once or twice, she even got a leading role—in B-minus movies. But that couldn't satisfy this California girl, and in 1946, she quit films.

If she had remained a star in retirement, she might be only a silvery soubrette in old-timers' memories, but a shadow on the modern screen. Yet today's moviegoers do recall Stuart, for she was old Rose, the elderly version of Kate Winslet's lovelorn aristocrat, in James Cameron's 1997 *Titanic.* Stuart was 86 when she played that part, but the character was 100. And when she died on Sept. 26 in a Los Angeles suburb, she was 100 too.

Joan Sutherland

LUCIANO PAVAROTTI ONCE CALLED Joan Sutherland "the greatest coloratura soprano of all time." Her fans in Italy agreed, calling her *"la Stupenda."* Others called her the successor to Maria Callas. The Australian was a late bloomer, but from the day she burst onto the international scene with a Lucia di Lammermoor at Covent Garden in 1959 until her retirement in 1990, she was renowned as a master of the difficult bel canto operas of Handel and others, and she helped lead their restoration to the repertoire. Sutherland died on Oct. 10 at 83.

Stuart